SerenDIPity
Celebrating Dips, Faith & Friendship

By Sharon E. Sloan

Faith and Sweet and Savory blessings!
Love,
Sharon
Psalm 27:4

SerenDIPity ~ Celebrating Dips, Faith & Friendship

© 2013 by Sharon Sloan

No portion of this book may be reproduced in any form without prior written permission.

ISBN-13: 978-1490909776
ISBN-10: 149090977X

SerenDIPity logo created by Tracy Stokes of Open Eye Design. Service Mark pending.

Scriptures taken from the Holy Bible, New International Version®, NIV®. Copyright © 1973, 1978, 1984, 2011 by Biblica, Inc.™ Used by permission of Zondervan. All rights reserved worldwide. www.zondervan.com The "NIV" and "New International Version" are trademarks registered in the United States Patent and Trademark Office by Biblica, Inc.™

Scriptures taken from the Holy Bible, New International Reader's Version®, NIrV® Copyright © 1995, 1996, 1998 by Biblica, Inc.™ Used by permission of Zondervan. www.zondervan.com The "NIrV" and "New International Reader's Version" are trademarks registered in the United States Patent and Trademark Office by Biblica, Inc.™

Scripture taken from the Amplified Bible, Copyright © 1954, 1958, 1962, 1964, 1965, 1987 by The Lockman Foundation. Used by permission.

Scripture quotations taken from the New American Standard Bible®, Copyright © 1960, 1962, 1963, 1968, 1971, 1972, 1973, 1975, 1977, 1995 by The Lockman Foundation. Used by permission.

Scriptures taken from the Holy Bible, some from the English Standard Version® (ESV®), copyright © 2001 by Crossway, a publishing ministry of Good News Publishers. Used by permission. All rights reserved.

Scripture quotations are taken from the Holy Bible, New Living Translation, copyright ©1996, 2004, 2007 by Tyndale House Foundation. Used by permission of Tyndale House Publishers, Inc., Carol Stream, Illinois 60188. All rights reserved.

Published in the United States of America

Layout by www.designbyinsight.net.

Dedication

*"Lord, You establish peace for us;
all that we have accomplished You have done for us.
O Lord, our God...Your name alone do we honor."*

~ Isaiah 26:12-13

Through this whimsical but sincere offering called "SerenDIPity", my heart's prayer is that God's Word and His Name will be exalted above all else and in all things. The Lord serendipitously inspired me with the idea for SerenDIPity. My desire is to honor Him and bring glory to His name. Anything I have accomplished, He has accomplished through me.

"...You have exalted above all things Your name and Your word." ~
Psalm 138:2

With deep gratitude to the Lord for each and every good gift He has given, this book is dedicated with big love to the family and friends with whom God has blessed our family ~

"A great group of people!"

This great group of people has made SerenDIPity dip parties so special.

One of the most meaningful compliments Jim and I received after a SerenDIPity party was from our friends Rich and Lisa who said the celebration was the gathering of "a great group of people". God has chosen for us and blessed us with loving family and amazing friends. For each unique one, we are forever thankful. We are humbled by His goodness to us.

> *"For a Christian, there are, strictly speaking, no chances. A secret Master of the Ceremonies has been at work. Christ, who said to the disciples 'Ye have not chosen me, but I have chosen you' can truly say to every group of Christian friends 'You have not chosen one another but I have chosen you for one another.' The Friendship is not a reward for our discrimination and good taste in finding one another out. It is the instrument by which God reveals to each the beauties of all the others." - CS Lewis*

And so this book is humbly and enthusiastically dedicated to the instruments by which God reveals to us His beauty ~ our family and friends ~ a great group of people who have graced us with their presence in our hearts and home.

You have made an indelible impression in our lives. You have doused us with love, and our hearts are dripping with thanks. You have splashed us with encouragement over and over, at just the right times. YOU, your creativity, your talents, your enthusiasm and your love have made SerenDIPity what it has become. You are loved. This offering called SerenDIPity book is dedicated to you. May His serendipitous blessings and pleasant surprises be yours in abundance! We are with you heart and soul!

> *"And his armor-bearer said to him, 'Do all that is in your heart. Do as you wish. Behold, I am with you heart and soul.'"*
>
> 1 Samuel 14:7 (ESV)

Special Thanks

To my husband, Jim, who is my sweetheart, my best friend, my confidante, my covering, my iron that sharpens iron, my challenger, my accountability partner and my cheerleader (in the manliest of ways). He is the anchor of our home and family.

Jim encouraged me several years ago to attend a Christian writer's and leadership conference called She Speaks (inspired by Proverbs 31:26). It made no sense to me at the time as I was busy raising two toddlers and just trying to keep my head above water. If I kept us all fed and breathing, I was happy at the end of the day. Attending a conference was not on my radar screen.

So I resisted Jim's gracious invitation to send me to the conference for a few years, but I finally attended and was blessed in the most serendipitous of ways. The Lord used that conference mostly to deepen my relationship with Him and to nurture my love for His Word. The Lord graciously introduced me to some amazing women who love and serve Him wholeheartedly with passion. The Lord also used that conference to direct my paths in specific ways. For that I am so thankful to the Lord and to Jim for their love and wisdom. www.shespeaksconference.com

Jim was the catalyst for me in taking the time to write this book. He felt I had something unique to share from and for the Lord. With his sweet insistence and love, I have completed this labor of love.

Jim has served as my editor for this book. He is smart and is a natural at editing. He gave me hours of intrinsic encouragement and support. More than anything, he has shown his confidence in me... not because of any good in me but because of what the Lord chooses to do through me, a broken and willing vessel.

"Her husband has full confidence in her and lacks nothing of value."
~ Proverbs 31:11

"I say to the LORD, 'You are my Lord;
apart from You I have no good thing.'"
~ Psalm 16:2

Thank you, Jim, for your belief that God has a plan and purpose for my life, for identifying His gifts in me and for cheering me on as I pursue Him with my whole heart. I respect you and I love you from the depths of my heart and soul.

And to our children, Joshua and Gabrielle, who have given us more joy and courage than we ever knew could fill our hearts. Thank you for loving a very imperfect mom who desires desperately to honor our completely perfect God. You represent His truth and grace to me in the most beautiful ways. I am humbled. I respect and love you very much.

"...grace and truth came through Jesus Christ."
~ John 1:17

Table of Contents

Dedication	3
Special Thanks	5
Chapter One: The Heart of Serendipity	11
Chapter Two: Opening Your Home ~ Hospitality	19
Chapter Three: Panache and Preparation	31
Chapter Four: Invitations ~ Setting The Stage	53
Chapter Five: Prizes and Pleasant Surprises!	65
Chapter Six: Only One Rule ~ No Double Dipping!	81
Chapter Seven: Savory Spoonfuls	91
Chapter Eight: Dollops of Dessert	105
Chapter Nine: SerenDIPity Afterglow	119

Ser-en-dip-i-ty [ser-*uh* n-dip-i-tee]
—*noun*
1. an unexpected desirable discovery
2. a pleasant surprise

(adapted from www.dictionary.com)

"When you have eaten and are satisfied,

*praise the L*ORD *your God…"*

~ Deuteronomy 8:10

Chapter 1

The Heart of Serendipity

"Serendipity occurs when something beautiful breaks into the monotonous and the mundane. A serendipitous life is marked by 'surprisability' and spontaneity. When we lose our capacity for either, we settle into life's ruts."
~ Charles R. Swindoll

Serendipity. It's one of my favorite words. One that brings warm memories to my heart.

I believe the SerenDIPity dip party is God's idea whispered into my heart. I know that might sound silly and even ridiculous to some. But my husband, Jim, and I believe it. When I am frequently asked the question, "Where did you get the idea for the SerenDIPity dip party?", my response is simply this: Our gracious and creative God gave me the idea.

SerenDIPity is a hospitality idea, a gathering for fellowship, food and friendship.

Jim and I love to gather friends together for fellowship, to nourish existing friendships, to introduce special friends from different circles to each other, and for new friendships to begin. That is my heart ~ gathering and growing together in the Lord and in friendship. It is an honor that tickles me when God gives me the blessing of introducing two people who then begin a sweet friendship of their own. And I am so thankful for the beautiful instruments of His grace in my life whom I call friends.

When I shared the idea of the SerenDIPity dip party with Jim, he was enthusiastic and excitedly said, "Let's do it!" As Jim and I prayed for God's blessing, presence and favor over this idea called "SerenDIPity", God answered our prayers beyond imagination. Honestly, I feel kind of selfish because Jim and I, and even our children, Joshua and Gabrielle, were so blessed though our desire was to bless others. Our hearts were full and content by HIS goodness. And beyond that, He has answered our prayers for our guests in so many ways. *"For surely, O LORD, You bless the righteous; You surround them with your favor as with a shield." Psalm 5:12*

At each SerenDIPity, our joy is hearing the laughter of our friends and feeling the warmth of sweet fellowship. Our hearts are filled having so much love under our roof and in our home. We are so very thankful to the Lord. *"We love because He first loved us." John 4:19*

One of the greatest pleasures of my heart is to gather family and friends together. Whether for a celebration, a Bible study or simply for fellowship, I love to gather together with loved ones. Friends have graciously told me that "gathering" is one of my unique God-given gifts. I heard a pastor once say that, in life, we either gather or we scatter. I am humbled and honored if I am a gatherer. *"He who is not with Me is against Me, and he who does not gather with Me scatters." ~ Luke 11:23*

Whether a dollop or a dousing, the sweet fellowship enveloped in gathering together in friendship satisfies a sweet spot in our God-breathed souls.

Small, intimate fellowship is a blessing. A one-on-one lunch with a girlfriend is something I cherish dearly. Having another family over for Sunday dinner is a blessing our family treasures. A face-to-face conversation with an extended family member is priceless. Intimate time and intimate moments build relationships in a special way. *"The LORD would speak to Moses face to face, as one speaks to a friend." ~ Exodus 33:11*

On the flip side of the gathering coin, I also enjoy hosting and planning parties. If we are going to party, then let's par-tae! I am big on birthday parties and love the opportunity to celebrate the lives of those with whom God has blessed us. When my husband and I were given our two children, Joshua and Gabrielle, we had all the more reason to celebrate and have enjoyed hosting birthday parties to celebrate their lives. I delight in preparing parties, whether very intimate or wonderfully large, to make momentous family occasions memorable and special.

When we are invited to a gathering with family and friends, we consider it a privilege to share in that celebration. Invitations speak of love, acceptance and care. Invitations are sacred in a sense, and we don't take it lightly when we receive such.

An Invitation That Changed My Life Forever

I received an invitation once that changed my life. And this invitation led me to the place where I first heard of the word serendipity. I like that the life-changing invitation and serendipity went together in my life! Here's the short version of my testimony.

My friend and next-door neighbor since birth, Leah, had a profound impact on my life. Though we grew up enjoying years of playing Chinese jump rope, Barbies and cards, it was an invitation she extended to me when I was in 9th grade that transformed my heart. Forever.

Leah invited me to attend her youth group that was simply called *Senior High*. A group of 9th – 12th graders gathered each Sunday evening for worship, Bible study, prayer and fellowship. There I made wonderful friendships, had loads of fun, and I fell in puppy love for the first time.

But most importantly, I began a life-long relationship with my First Love, Jesus.

Through this youth group to which Leah invited me and a Bible study I attended on Friday evenings with my mom, God lovingly revealed my sin to me and my need for the Savior. He drew me to Himself and I received Jesus as Savior and Lord. Only by His grace.

And in His goodness, God drew me to Himself at a critical time in my young life -- just in the midst of the awkward years of junior high and high school! He saved me from many poor choices that could have devastated my life. He also tenderly reached out to me during a time in my life when my parents separated in their marriage. Though I knew both of my parents loved me deeply and I didn't misunderstand their individual and marital issues as something personal against or about me, my heart was still saddened and my family was broken. By God's sweet mercy and grace, He gave me wisdom, discernment and understanding beyond my years concerning my parents' separation. I needed His perfect provision during that season of life. I know that His love and faithfulness have sustained each person in my family, and for that I am so grateful. And my heart is eternally humbled and thankful that He kindly and lovingly knocked on the door of my heart at the most tender of times. Titus 3:4-7 is my life salvation verse.

> *"But when the kindness and love of God our Savior appeared, He saved us, not because of righteous things we had done, but because of His mercy. He saved us through the washing of rebirth and renewal by the Holy Spirit, whom He poured out on us generously through Jesus Christ our Savior, so that, having been justified by His grace, we might become heirs having the hope of eternal life."*
> *~ Titus 3:4-7*

Taste and See That The Lord Is Good

If you have not heard the Gospel of Christ and received Him as Savior yet, I invite you to do so right now. It is really the matter of first importance to me, my husband and my family.

> *"For what I received I passed on to you as of first importance: that Christ died for our sins according to the Scriptures, that He was buried, that He was raised on the third day according to the Scriptures…"*
> *~ 1 Corinthians 15:3-4*

If you read no further in this book, I would be thrilled for you to stop right here and give your heart and life to Jesus. I invite you to meet our life-redeeming, heart-changing Savior. He loves you and desires a personal, intimate relationship with you! You are the apple of His eye.

> *"…for whoever touches you touches the apple of His eye…"*
> *~Zechariah 2:8*

Click here to learn more: http://peacewithgod.jesus.net/

> *"Oh, taste and see that the Lord is good;*
> *Blessed is the man who trusts in Him!"*
> *~ Psalm 34:8*

The Lord wants to dine with you. That's the best invitation you will ever receive! He's knocking…open the door of your heart and invite Him in.

> *"Behold, I stand at the door and knock. If anyone hears My voice and opens the door, I will come in to him and dine with him, and he with Me."*
> *~ Revelation 3:20 (NKJV)*

If you have received this invitation of salvation through Jesus Christ today, I would love to hear from you. Please feel free to email me at sharon@serendipitydipsbook.com.

"You shall be filled at My table…"
~ Ezekiel 39:20

"You still the hunger of those you cherish; their sons have plenty, and they store up wealth for their children."
~ Psalm 17:14

When I First Heard The Word "Serendipity"

The youth group I was attending with my friend, Leah, would occasionally have mini-retreats called "Serendipity", at which we would stay overnight at the church. We would have special devotion time, encourage friends in the Lord and play lots of spirited games. We would stay up late and get up early. The Serendipity was filled with surprise blessings from each other and from the Lord. These Serendipities made a lasting impression on me that still leave a sweet and savory flavor in my heart today.

I had never heard the whimsical word "Serendipity" before those youth group mini-retreats, but the way it sounded, the definition and the warm memories from the Sr. High Youth Group Serendipity mini-retreats soon made it one of my favorite words in the English language. ("Autumnal" is another favorite word of mine, but that is a story and book for another day.)

The First SerenDIPity Dip Party

In 2009, I was inspired to put a culinary twist on the word SerenDIPity and make it a celebration ~ a gathering of family and friends where all DIPS were served. Savory and sweet dips – appetizers and desserts – would be the posh nosh for the celebration.

Though a sit-down or buffet dinner is always enjoyable, noshing on a variety of appetizers excites my taste buds! Our guests – ladies and gentlemen – enjoy dipping the evening away and filling themselves with great food and fellowship. The plethora of dip flavors and textures adds a culinary depth to the SerenDIPity celebration. And the assortments of food selections and culinary creations are also effortless conversation starters between new friends and with tried and true friends.

I am a cheerleader by nature. And though I am not competitive, I do love encouraging and gift-giving (the spiritual gift of giving scored as one of my top two in a Spiritual Gift Assessment). So, while we were at it, why not add a little fun to the party and give away gifts and prizes at SerenDIPity? The light-hearted competition has added an extra layer of fun to the gathering.

Surprisability is major fun factor in SerenDIPity!! It is fun to plan little surprises before, during and after SerenDIPity that bless your guests. We'll explore this a little more later in the book.

When I shared my vision of the SerenDIPity dip party with Jim, he was heartily all for it. So in 2010, we hosted our first SerenDIPity. Having received sweet compliments and encouragement from friends to continue SerenDIPity and make it an annual tradition, we have done so. It is really fun to see how our friends share their enthusiasm and excitement about SerenDIPity, often on the lookout for new recipes and presentation ideas throughout the year for the next SerenDIPity dip party.

We have had several guests sweetly tell us that SerenDIPity is their favorite party and social highlight of the year. So in the love and spirit of Acts 4:32, I want to share this idea with you and encourage you to host your own SerenDIPity.

"All the believers were one in heart and mind. No one claimed that any of his possessions was his own, but they shared everything they had."

~ Acts 4:32

Of course, you can add your own twists to SerenDIPity and should tailor it to your personality. I will give you our basics, and you can add or subtract from there to create your own flavor of SerenDIPity.

SerenDIPity serves up tasty unexpected blessings in fellowship, friendship and food. So grab a spoon and prepare to dip in and enjoy!

Chapter 2

Opening Your Home
~ Hospitality

"As Jesus and His disciples were on their way, He came to a village where a woman named Martha opened her home to Him." – Luke 10:38 (NIV)

Opening our homes to others. This simple act of kindness and hospitality was important enough that it was noted in scripture when Martha opened her home to Jesus. Martha gets a bum rap from Christians about being too busy to sit at the feet of Jesus, and I agree she totally needed to slow down and first spend significant and meaningful time with the Savior, **as do we** on a daily basis. Her priorities needed to be realigned in the example of her we see in scripture. Yet I always want to remember the great example Martha was in that she beautifully and easily opened her home, and therefore her heart, to Jesus. The KJV says "she welcomed Him into her house". I like that. And I remember Matthew 25:40, that however we serve others in His name, we are serving Him. *"**The King will reply, 'Truly I tell you, whatever you did for one of the least of these brothers and sisters of mine, you did for Me.'**"*

Yet, this simple act of hospitality can seem so complicated, so overwhelming, so stressful and even so unnecessary in our lives today.

The art and heart of entertaining seem to be waning in this world of social media, where, if we are not disciplined and resolved, most of our social interaction can be in front of a computer or smart phone screen instead of face-to-face. *"The LORD spoke to you face to face…" ~ Deuteronomy 5:4*

Our busy and technology-driven lives contribute to our lack of personal fellowship one with another. Opening our homes and inviting others in for coffee, snacks, a meal or a party can easily slip off our heart's and calendar's radar screens. But I believe we are called and commanded to be hospitable in whatever form the Lord chooses. *"And let us not neglect our meeting together, as some people do, but encourage one another.." ~ Hebrews 10:25*

Serving For God's Glory

"But the end of all things is at hand; therefore be serious and watchful in your prayers. And above all things have fervent love for one another, for 'love will cover a multitude of sins.' Be hospitable to one another without grumbling. As each one has received a gift, minister it to one another, as good stewards of the manifold grace of God. If anyone speaks, let him speak as the oracles of God. If anyone ministers, let him do it as with the ability which God supplies, that in all things God may be glorified through Jesus Christ, to whom belong the glory and the dominion forever and ever. Amen."

– 1 Peter 4:7-11

Verses seven to eleven in First Peter are subtitled "Serving for God's Glory" in my New King James Version of the Bible. I find it interesting that in the list of things commanded of us in this passage are: to be serious (sober), to be prayerful, to be watchful, to be loving, to be hospitable without grumbling and to be faithful to use the gifts God has given us… "with the ability God supplies, that in all things God may be glorified through Jesus Christ, to whom belong the glory"!

Opening Your Home ~ Hospitality

Throughout scripture, God tells us to be hospitable. (To do a little topical study yourself, click here: http://www.openbible.info/topics/hospitality.) And did you notice in the passage above that we are to be hospitable "without complaining"! Wow!

Be hospitable without complaining. Let's break this down.

Be hospitable.

Without complaining.

The NLT says "cheerfully share your home".

I am moved that the God of the universe has made a clear point in scriptures that we know, respect and demonstrate the value of hospitality. Opening our hearts and homes to others deepens our relationships. It pleases God and it illustrates in living color John 13:35 ~ ***"By this everyone will know that you are my disciples, if you love one another."***

> *"God's plan is that when people watch our lives, they should see a true reflection of His nature in us. That's why Jesus prayed for His followers just before He went to the cross: 'that they may all be one; even as Thou, Father, art in Me, and I in Thee, that they also may be in Us.' (John 17:21). Jesus clearly expresses in the very next statement of His prayer that the believability of the Gospel message will depend on our unity among each other: "that the world may believe that Thou didst send Me" (John 17:21). It's a very sobering truth. We generally think that preaching confirmed by healing and miracles will cause people to believe in Jesus. But now we discover in Jesus' prayer that unless God's work is backed up by our unity, we actually destroy the credibility of the Gospel. That should alarm us enough to honestly examine our home life, our teamwork and our relationships with our husband, co-workers, leaders and church members."*

~ *Gisela Yohannan (Dear Sisters ~ Letters of Hope and Encouragement)*

Romans 12 (or "R-12" as it is sometimes called) is often referred to as the "relationship chapter". Romans 12 sums up beautifully how we are to serve the Lord and honor Him in our relationships through our behavior and our responses, both of which pour forth from our hearts. In the middle of this important chapter, God is sure to remind us that we are to be hospitable.

Does that grab your heart a bit? It grabs mine.

God values and honors hospitality.

In Romans 12:13 NKJV, we are told to be "given to hospitality". The ESV Bible states Romans 12:13 this way: "Contribute to the needs of the saints and seek to show hospitality."

Seek to show hospitality. Am I seeking ways I can show hospitality? These four words in scripture are very challenging.

I got curious and looked up this scripture in the Amplified Bible which says "pursue the practice of hospitality". Let's take a look together. Here's a quick glance at Romans 12:13 from the Parallel Bible:

NKJV – "…given to hospitality"
NIV – "Practice hospitality."
NLT – "Always be eager to practice hospitality."
ESV – "…seek to show hospitality"
HCS – "pursue hospitality"
AMP – "pursue the practice of hospitality"

Clearly put, we are to be hospitable and open our homes to others. We are all in varying situations and seasons of our lives, so being hospitable and opening your home to others may look different for each of us at any given time. Whether it is a simple act of offering someone a cup of cold water or entertaining a large group of people, being hospitable reflects a part of the heart of God.

Opening Your Home ~ Hospitality

Your Home ~ A Gift From The Master

"Hospitality seeks to minister. It says, 'This home is not mine. It is truly a gift from my Master. I am His servant and I use it as He desires.' Hospitality does not try to impress, but to serve."

- Karen Burton Mains

Jim and I were married six years and living in a condo before we purchased our single home. We both worked full-time and wanted to decrease our debt and increase our savings before we purchased a home. When we were ready to make the financial commitment to buy a house, we carefully looked at existing homes and also new construction. We didn't have children at the time, and so we were in no hurry to choose a house and move in. We knew our budget and how much we could afford to spend on a home. We spent a year searching for just the right home. We house hunted from one end of our county in Pennsylvania to another. We would often spend enjoyable Sunday afternoons touring new construction sample homes or at open houses for existing homes. Like choosing a wedding gown, I knew I would know the right one when I saw it and tried it on for size. And after one year, the Lord introduced us to our home.

"...He determined the times set for them and the exact places where they should live."

~ Acts 17:26

We just happened to be cutting through a neighborhood in the town in which we lived. I noticed a "for sale" sign being put in the ground in front of a pretty house. I asked Jim if we could call our realtor to request an appointment to see the house. Jim gently and wisely reminded me that a home in this neighborhood was not likely in our price range. But something inside of me just wanted to see it. I asked Jim again and he agreed.

Jim called our realtor, who repeated Jim's sentiments almost verbatim, *"It is above your price range. There is no sense in looking at it."* But that nudge inside of my heart was persistent. Jim and our realtor agreed, and the following evening we met to walk through the house.

As soon as we walked in, I loved it. Like trying on the right wedding gown, this house fit perfectly. It felt right. And Jim loved it, too. Each room we walked through got better and better. The woman of the house had just recently re-modeled everything in the house without her or her husband knowing that the company for which he worked was going to offer him a promotion and relocation package to another state. An immaculately-kept home with fresh paint, new wall coverings, recently-laid carpets and brand spanking new tile in the kitchen made this a move-in mint condition home. The backyard opened up into acres of protected open space that the family could enjoy, but which was maintained and mowed by the neighborhood's homeowner's association.

Perfect scenario.

Jim, our realtor and I finished looking through the inside and outside of the home and said good-bye to the homeowners. I remember the three of us then stood on the driveway talking for quite a while. Jim and I both felt the same excitement about the house…except for the asking price, which was well above our price range. But the gentle nudge was still there in my heart.

"Can we just make an offer of what we can afford in our price range? Can we just try?" I asked. Jim and our realtor both thought making our offer would be futile. Moreover, our realtor said, *"Sharon, this is my career, my business, my industry. Your offer is way too low, and I would actually be embarrassed as a professional to put in your offer. There is no way it will be accepted."* But the nudge quietly said, *"Can we still try?"*

More because the men felt sorry for me than anything else, our realtor humbly agreed and submitted our very low offer the next day. A few days passed and we heard nothing back. I remember sitting at my desk at the law firm for which I worked as a paralegal at the time staring at the phone. Hoping it would ring with Jim's voice or our realtor's voice on the other end of my extension, I prayed to God for His will. My heart was sinking that we hadn't heard a word from the seller's realtor…not even a rejection or a slammed door in our faces. Hope was waning.

Then the phone call came. The receptionist put the call through to me. It was our realtor.

"Sharon, you are not going to believe this. The husband who owns this house with his wife was given an unexpected promotion which requires the family to move to Chicago. The pharmaceutical company for which he works wants him out there as soon as possible. Because they want him to move quickly and not still be concerned with selling his home, the pharmaceutical company is paying the sellers the thousands of dollars difference between your offer and their asking price. The only thing they are asking is for you to pay $1,000 for the brand new shed they just had put in the backyard. They are taking your offer, Sharon."

Thousands of dollars difference from our offer and their asking price. They took our offer. The husband's pharmaceutical company paid the difference. God's provision. God knows the exact places we are to live.

Our home is His home.

From that first moment, we dedicated our home to the Lord. We promised to use it for ministry as He leads and for His glory and purposes. God gave us this house. We open it up for Bible studies, ministry, fellowship and hospitality whenever He leads us.

I love the quote by Karen Burton Mains at the beginning of this chapter, which my dear friend, Heather, shared with me. *"Hospitality seeks to minister. It says, 'This home is not mine. It is truly a gift from my Master. I am His servant and I use it as He desires.' Hospitality does not try to impress, but to serve."*

Our home is not ours. It is truly a gift from our Master. We are His servants, and we want to use it as He desires. We desire to serve others. We desire to bless, not impress.

"As for me and my house, we will serve the Lord."
~ Joshua 24:15

To some our home is modest and small, to others it may be spacious and grand. Either way, to us it is just right. It is what the Lord has provided for us. And we want to open the door of our home to guests. God has made a point of its importance through scripture, so we know there will be fruit for His purposes as we swing wide open the door of our hearts and house to family, friends and even strangers.

The beauty of the house is order;
The blessing of the house is contentment;
The glory of the house is hospitality;
The crown of the house is godliness.
~ Anonymous

The Fruit of Opening Your Home

"By wisdom a house is built, and through understanding it is established; through knowledge its rooms are filled with rare and beautiful treasures."
~ Proverbs 24:3-4

Opening our homes in hospitality usually involves stepping out of our comfort zones. Whether we are preparing a meal to bring to someone or inviting others to our home, it often involves a surrender of selfishness. But as we yield to God's leading through being hospitable, He fills our hearts with joy and gives us the blessing of tasting and seeing that He is indeed good.

"Taste and see that the Lord is good..."
~Psalm 34:8

To really spur you on and encourage you to open up your home if this is not normally something you do, I want to share with you just a few of the sweet comments, notes and emails we have received from friends who have been guests at SerenDIPity. Jim and I prayerfully share these with you to inspire you to open your home in hospitality and to point to the good fruit He brings when we do.

Whether you decide to host a SerenDIPity or simply open your home in another way and invite guests in, you are taking an important step in building and nourishing friendships. And best of all, you are honoring God and obeying His Word to practice hospitality. ***"How good and pleasant it is when God's people live together in unity! For there the Lord bestows His blessing, even life forevermore." – Psalm 133:1, 3***

> *"Our homes are so often a reflection of our hearts, and when they are opened up and offered to others, something wonderful happens. Entertaining should reflect the host/hostess and the desire to gather people together to make memories and build lasting friendships. SerenDIPity has taken the usual party to a whole new level. We enjoy light-hearted competition, laughter, eating and the company of friends in the relaxed comfort of a home. For me, SerenDIPity is a return to the lost art of entertaining with the heart of Christian hospitality at its center. The wonderful whimsy of SerenDIPity is the icing on the cake!"*
>
> *~ Lucille*

> *"SerenDIPity's greatest blessings for me are the friendships that have grown from and through it. As you open your home, it is like a flowerbed and your guests are the flowers. SerenDIPity tenderly gathers us all together. SerenDIPity feeds us with kindness, showers us with the love of God and warms us with sweet hospitality. Through all of this, strong friendships have grown that are rooted in the word of God. Ken and I are so blessed to be a part of this blossoming annual event."*
>
> *~ Erika*

SerenDIPity: Celebrating Dips, Faith & Friendship

"Thanks again for opening your home through SerenDIPity and for having me and Lisa last evening for another year of SerenDIPity. It is my favorite celebration of the year, except for Christmas and Easter. I didn't eat all day yesterday just waiting for the dipping to begin. We had a blast with everyone and a ton of fun. The down side today is that dippy is over for this year. The up side is that it is only 364 days until the next SerenDIPity."

~ Rich

~~~~~~~

"We are delighted to be joining in the festivities of the most serendipitous kind. We thank you for your invitation and are so looking forward to gathering with friends at the most spectacular evening of the year. With thanksgiving in our hearts…and visions of sugar plums and 'manly dip' dancing in our heads."

~ Steven and Deborah B.

~~~~~~~

"Thank you for opening your home and for prayerfully connecting us with friends. Your SerenDIPity has become a much-anticipated celebration each year. The heart of your SerenDIPity is the fellowship, the companionship, the community. It is the purity of this gathering that makes it so special for Rob and me. There is something so unique about SerenDIPity and how you open your home to friends and family. There is no pretense, no standing on ceremony, just you simply joining people together for the sheer pleasure of community, laughter, friendship, love of good food, love of good people, love of Jesus. Even if your guests don't know Jesus, for sure they will feel His presence at a gathering that has been covered in prayer and bathed in love. I love the simplicity…

Opening Your Home ~ Hospitality

people getting together simply to love on each other. And the icing on the cake? Folks bring their "A game", getting creative and whipping up dips and displays to bring about giggles and to treat taste buds. But surely the best part of the evening are exceptional people brought together for a memorable celebration. I am already ready to put next year's date on the calendar!"

~ Heather

"SerenDIPity was an AMAZING party! There are so many delicious foods and unbelievable deserts made by your guests! It is like no other party I have attended in the past…so creative! Thank you so much for making everyone feel special and at ease! We really enjoyed the party! Thanks for opening your home and for inviting us!"

~ Yang

"Thank you for opening your home and inviting us to SerenDIPity. We look forward to it so much and it is one of the social highlights of our year. It is so wonderful to gather with friends and enjoy adult conversation and fellowship that enriches our relationships. We have so much fun in the weeks ahead of SerenDIPity as we look for a new recipe to bring for the casual and enjoyable competition. We love SerenDIPity."

~ Kevin and Penny

SerenDIPity: Celebrating Dips, Faith & Friendship

"Thank you for opening your home and inviting us to SerenDIPity. The hospitality of SerenDIPity has meant so much to us that we look forward to it all year. We always feel so loved and welcomed as we enjoy the intimate fellowship and amazing food. It makes me feel connected to my family in Christ. The ultimate in warmth and hospitality, everyone who enters your home feels Jesus's love and yours!"

~ Sean and Jen

~~~~~~

*"Give me neither poverty nor riches;
feed me with the food that is needful for me…"*

~ Proverbs 30:8

We pray these snippets have pointed you to His word and that you are challenged and encouraged to open your home and invite others in for fellowship! The Lord will bless your heart. My prayer for you is that He will show you His favor and that He will establish and bless the work of your heart and hands as you reach out to others in hospitality.

*"May the favor of the Lord our God rest on us;
establish the work of our hands for us—
yes, establish the work of our hands."*

~ Psalm 90:17

CHAPTER 3

Panache and Preparation

"As water reflects the face, so one's life reflects the heart."
~ Proverbs 27:19

Panache ~ Your Own Style!

SerenDIPity should represent your own flair! Your celebration represents your passions, your joys and your hospitality style. For me, I like to mix the whimsical and the elegant together. Light-hearted, comfortable whimsy and a splash of bold elegance let my guests know they are special and make for a memorable celebration of faith, dips and friendships.

My Personal Twist

One word that represents one of my passions: SHOES! I love shoes. Cute and stylish shoes. Not expensive shoes, mind you. Just unique and fashionable shoes…especially those with heels and any kind of animal print or involving the color purple. I know you may be asking, "What do shoes have to do with this?", but somehow it just happened. Serendipity.

The shoe twist was not one that I planned or even thought about. It just happened! At our first SerenDIPity, our lovely hostess assistant, Jill, wore FABULOUS shoes. Yes, that's right…cheetah pumps. (Girlfriends who get this, stand up and say "stilettos"!) Jill's cheetah print pumps set off a spark of shoe conversation fireworks. It was very fun. So, we serendipitously began giving little awards for cute shoes. (Read more about this in Chapter 5 - "Prizes and Pleasant Surprises".)

Jill's fabulous shoes from SerenDIPity 2010
(Photo by Heather Beals)

Panache and Preparation

Jim's Personal Twist

Our dear friends, Cheryl and Wade, brought this very manly chipped beef creation to SerenDIPity 2013. It was perfect for dipping crackers in and certainly won Jim's vote!

(Photo by Toni Valentini)

Jim's only stated requirement to me when we hosted our first SerenDIPity was that it wasn't all "girly food". He was hoping for hearty, carnivorous dips…not just carrot sticks with low-fat ranch dip. Over the years, manly dip contributions have become a fun game-changing part of our SerenDIPity. So, for instance, one way we show our own style is that Jim awards "Manly Prizes" for manly dips. This fun twist represents his personality and passions well. Our friends Mike and Lynne stepped up to the plate big time their first year and brought a big tray of cheese, pepperoni and a variety of mustards for dipping. It was simple yet very satisfying. Needless to say, they took home a prize from Jim for their manly contribution.

SerenDIPity: Celebrating Dips, Faith & Friendship

Lynne and Mike's "Manly Meat, Mustard and Cheese" from SerenDIPity 2011 (Photograph by Megan Brock)

In response to Jim's honest request for guests to "man up" so to speak and not just bring girly food, one of our guests, Steven, brings Jim a fabulous manly host gift each year – a t-bone steak from our local farmer's market! Steven really knows how to bond with Jim! The host gift is always a treat for Jim.

Think of your own personality and passions and how you can incorporate them into your SerenDIPity party! Consider your guests and be sure there is a twist for the women and the men.

Preparation

Once you have a vision for your own SerenDIPity party, you can begin preparing. Now that SerenDIPity is an annual event for us, I prepare here and there throughout the year as I think of something or as I happen upon a great clearance sale for party goods or culinary-related prizes. (Again, SerenDIPity is what you make it. Gifts and prizes are definitely optional and are not required! We'll talk more about that later.)

Here is a general timeline for my preparations. Use this as a guideline and tailor it to your own personality and how you work best. I tend to work best well ahead of deadlines. I don't like being late or feeling the pressure of unpreparedness. That's just my personality. I believe preparation means PREparation! Pre means before. And I will be honest…I get grumpy when I feel overwhelmed, so preparing ahead is wise and loving self-preservation for me and my sweet family. Smiles. I don't like when I am grumpy toward my family (and neither do they)!

Time Frame	Action Item
Three Months Ahead	Set Date/Mark Your Calendar Plan Party Budget (with spouse if married)
10 Weeks Ahead	Email or send Save-The-Date cards
8-10 Weeks Ahead	Make a list of any home improvements you would like to accomplish before the SerenDIPity. Take action to be sure these are completed in time.

6-8 Weeks Ahead	Send Invitations (include blank recipe cards) Secure any hostess assistants and/or photographer you will want for the evening
6 Weeks Ahead	Begin shopping for good deals on party paper products, party favors, disposable containers, plastic wrap, aluminum foil and prizes (optional)
4 Weeks Ahead	Get your dip recipes together and make a grocery list of the items you will need to purchase
1-2 Weeks Ahead	Wrap prizes/Prepare party favors Review RSVP responses Gather electric cords, serving utensils and other practical items you will need
Day Before/Day Of	Grocery shop, prepare dips, clean out Refrigerator and clean the house Relax and have fun dipping!

Even in being well-prepared ahead of time, there is always so much to do in the final days and hours of entertaining in your home. So the more that is done well ahead of time, the better off for everyone. Think, plan and prepare ahead as much as possible. It makes for a smoother entertaining day and a lovelier time for you and your guests.

Panache and Preparation

Setting The Date

When choosing your date for SerenDIPity, choose a date that will give you some breathing room before and after. You want to enjoy preparing for your guests beforehand, and you want time to enjoy the afterglow and clean up without stress the day after. Leave enough margin. Before selecting your date, see what other social events, holidays and obligations you already have scheduled. Consider the activities of your children, such as sporting games, practices, dance recitals, tournaments, etc. Try to pick a day where you are completely free for a few days before and for cleanup the day after. Then keep the days open so you do not become overwhelmed. (Have I mentioned that I tend to get cranky when I am feeling overwhelmed?) We have had our SerenDIPities during the late winter or very early spring weeks. These tend to be less busy and people enjoy getting out.

Once you have chosen your date, if you are married, be sure that you and your spouse go over the calendar together so you are on the same page. If your children are living at home, let them know about the party and what expectations you may have of them. Also let them know about party preparations and how your several days before will largely be spent on preparing for the party. When we communicate our goals and expectations, everyone can be in unity and it makes for a more enjoyable party planning and hosting experience. Amen?

Mark your calendar (whether it is the one on your refrigerator or the one in your mobile device) with the SerenDIPity date. Mark off the day before and the day after as your "breathing room dates". Write in any days in the week ahead that you want to keep open for preparation and cleaning. Set reminders for your "To Do" list. Keeping smart time boundaries around SerenDIPity will keep you cool and not feeling overwhelmed.

SerenDIPity Budget

Entertaining, whether plain or fancy, small or large, generally requires some kind of spending, even if minimal. Before planning your SerenDIPity, sit down and plan your budget so you can entertain reasonably and graciously without over-spending or accruing credit card debt. If you are married, sit with your spouse and discuss the party budget and write down how much you can spend on items such as paper goods, invitations, stamps, beverages, food, party favors (optional) and prizes (optional). If your vision for SerenDIPity is big but your budget is saying keep it small, then keep it small. Honoring God in obedience concerning spending is more important. *"To obey is better than sacrifice…" (1 Samuel 15:22)*

Possible Budget Items to Consider

- Paper Products (plates, napkins, plastic utensils, cold cups, hot cups)
- Invitations (you can save money by doing online invitations)
- Stamps (if mailing traditional invitations)
- Groceries/Food/Beverages/Ice
- Decorations (optional)
- Gifts/Prizes/Awards (optional)
- Party Favors (optional)
- Hostess Assistants (optional)
- Photographer (optional)
- Home improvement items (if necessary and able)

Entertaining does not have to be expensive. Clearance sales, wholesale markets, dollar stores and overstock stores are great resources for party goods, favors and prizes. You can begin saving for a

Panache and Preparation

party budget months ahead of time and be looking for deals whenever you are out shopping. It is important that you entertain without overspending and incurring debt. Celebrations are meant to bring joy and unity in your home and marriage, not strife and disharmony.

Also while planning your budget, consider having hostess assistants help you at SerenDIPity. This is a blessing that goes two ways: 1.) you can enjoy your guests, the fellowship, the festivities, and the dips all the more; and 2.) your hostess assistants earn money and gain experience.

We budget resources to hire high school students for the evening. And every year of SerenDIPity we have had Jim's cousin's lovely daughter be our Head Hostess Assistant. Jill effortlessly stepped into this role and made it her own. She does a fabulous job and knows what to do without me even saying a word. Her talents and diligence afford Jim and I the blessing of a relaxed and enjoyable celebration. Find a treasure like Jill for your Head Hostess Assistant.

Our fabulous Head Hostess Assistant ~ Jill
(Photo by Megan Brock)

Save-The-Date Cards/emails

Letting your guests know up to 10 weeks ahead of time to save the date for your SerenDIPity is a courtesy that will bless them. They will mark their calendars and keep the date open, if possible. They will look forward to SerenDIPity and begin thinking about and enjoy researching what dip they will bring. You can send a Save-The-Date via email free of charge. There are also online sites that send creative Save-The-Dates free of charge, such as www.punchbowl.com and www.paperlesspost.com. If you prefer sending traditional paper Save-The-Dates in the mail and have it in your budget to do so, go for it. I have often found these at clearance sales at our local Hallmark card stores.

Home Improvements/Housekeeping Preparations

"By wisdom a house is built, and through understanding it is established; through knowledge its rooms are filled with rare and beautiful treasures."

~ Proverbs 24:3-4

If your home is in excellent condition most of the time, this section may not apply to you, so feel free to skip this section altogether. I applaud you and rejoice with you if your home is spring-cleaned year round and you are a home fashion diva. I am not. So this section applies to me, and I imagine, to some of you as well.

I don't want to put unnecessary pressure on myself or you about the appearance and cleanliness of your home, other than to encourage you to honor well the home God has given you. I keep my heart and mind focused on the truth that our homes are filled with intangible rare and beautiful treasures when we fill it with love, wisdom, understanding and knowledge. We can all fill our homes with the most precious riches of all – His!

Panache and Preparation

I love my home and I keep it generally clean, neat and relatively stylish. I know our home is a gift from God and I do my best to honor Him by being a good housekeeper. However, I am not a visionary with interior design. I know what I like and don't like in the way of home interiors, but I can't walk into a room and envision a completely remodeled and updated space. I have a healthy taste in interiors, but I lack a keen sense of vision. Thankfully, I have a few dear friends or mentors who have fabulous vision for home interiors. They graciously help me…and they love doing it! Ask one of your friends who are gifted in this area to lend you a hand. They will be delighted.

Also, I sometimes have a shortage of wherewithal to forge ahead on home improvements to completion. Sometimes I feel as though, once you unearth one thing in order to improve it, a thousand other things are unearthed along with it that require your attention. Remember that *I don't deal well with feeling overwhelmed* thing? Enter crankiness when too many things are unearthed at once that require my attention! I can become discouraged and lose steam.

Home improvements can be overwhelming to me. I can bite off small pieces at a time and be productive. However, when we start addressing re-painting several rooms, updating decorating themes, replacing floors and making even small structural changes, I nearly faint! I want to be a good steward over my home, but I don't want to be consumed by it.

I am more relationship-oriented than task-oriented. Given the choice to accomplish tasks or spend meaningful time with someone I love, I will almost always pick the relationship. Though I consider myself to be productive, faithful and responsible, I generally feel that relationship choices usually have more eternal value than completing a task. This isn't always the case, of course. God wants us to be busy with our hands, our hearts and our minds. I just sometimes have trouble prioritizing dusting out my curio cabinet ahead of a date night with my husband or cheering my child on at a game or having lunch with a girlfriend.

Here's the great news for those of you like me: ***Entertaining is a great motivator for accomplishing home improvement goals we tend to put off.*** Setting goals for paying attention to housekeeping or home improvement items gets me moving. Entertaining and having people over helps me tend to things I might ordinarily place as a lower priority. This can range from things like dusting ceiling fans, washing baseboards with hot soapy water, or replacing an old plastic trash can with a new stainless steel one to stripping old wallpaper, spackling and painting walls in fresh new colors or replacing a sofa that has the stuffing coming out of it. Nothing like the goal of entertaining people I love motivates me to joyfully tend to these things that I would normally put on the back burner. But because my ultimate goal in accomplishing these tasks blesses my family and our guests, I am filled with satisfaction.

Write a list of housekeeping items and a separate list of home improvement projects you would like to complete before entertaining. Housekeeping items can usually be accomplished with little to no spending. Just perspiration and determination! For home improvement items that require spending, estimate the amount needed next to the item. Prayerfully see if your budget allows for home improvement projects. Often we only complete a few of them and decide some of them can wait until another time. Again, having the goal of entertaining is a motivator in completing tasks we might normally neglect or put off. Allow SerenDIPity to spur you on to love and good works! ***"Let us think of ways to motivate one another to acts of love and good works." ~ Hebrews 10:24 (NLT)***

Panache and Preparation

Secure and Hire Hostess Assistants and/or Photographer

"She gets up while it is still night; she provides food for her family and portions for her female servants."

~ Proverbs 31:15

Did you read this scripture? Female servants! The NLT Bible says "servant girls"! It is totally okay for you to ask for assistance and even hire help when needed! As a matter of fact, scripture encourages it. I call it the "Jethro Clause". Looky here:

"Moses' father-in-law [Jethro] replied, 'What you are doing is not good. You and these people who come to you will only wear yourselves out. The work is too heavy for you; you cannot handle it alone. Listen now to me and I will give you some advice, and may God be with you. You must be the people's representative before God and bring their disputes to him. Teach them his decrees and instructions, and show them the way they are to live and how they are to behave. But select capable men from all the people—men who fear God, trustworthy men who hate dishonest gain—and appoint them as officials over thousands, hundreds, fifties and tens. Have them serve as judges for the people at all times, but have them bring every difficult case to you; the simple cases they can decide themselves. That will make your load lighter, because they will share it with you. If you do this and God so commands, you will be able to stand the strain, and all these people will go home satisfied.' Moses listened to his father-in-law and did everything he said. He chose capable men from all Israel and made them leaders of the people, officials over thousands, hundreds, fifties and tens. They served as judges for the people at all times. The difficult cases they brought to Moses, but the simple ones they decided themselves."

~ Exodus 18:17-26

Having trustworthy and capable people to assist you will lighten your load, and as the passage in Exodus 18 states, "the people will go home satisfied." Woo hoo!

Hostess Assistants

As mentioned previously, we have had hostess assistants for our SerenDIPities. To keep within entertaining budget, we hire high school students who are friendly, conscientious and responsible. We pay them a reasonable yet generous amount and they are delighted to earn that money. They also gain experience working by serving and cleaning up, and they grow by socializing with our adult guests. Having the hostess assistants shines a whole different light on the evening as the host and hostess, freeing us up to enjoy the festivities. Hostess assistants also enhance your guests' experience as well. Here are some ideas of how to best utilize your assistants.

Head Hostess Assistant

- Knows the overall vision for the evening and responsibilities of all assistants
- Gently oversees the activities of hostess assistants
- Takes initiative to care for things that would be done by the host and hostess
- Records the dips as guests arrive, assigns each dip a number, writes a dip name card
- Collects recipe cards as guests arrive
- Collects Grand Prize tickets when guests arrive (if applicable)
- Oversees the tallying of the votes and records the stats and winners
- Assists in serving and clean up throughout the evening

Hostess Assistants

- Take jackets and coats from guests and hangs or stores them in assigned area
- Help place dips in their appropriate place for display and tasting
- Assist guests who need serving utensils or plates/bowls for their dips
- Refill cold beverage stations and decorative water dispensers as needed
- Refresh ice buckets as needed
- Keep paper good and plastic utensils stocked
- Keep hot beverages stocked, including cream and sweeteners
- Place dips in their assigned area
- Clean up spills and throw used paper goods away
- Replace trash bags in trash cans and empty recycles as they fill
- Assist in clean up at the end of the evening

We are so thankful for our hostess assistants and find it very wise and beneficial to have them as an integral part of a successful SerenDIPity.

Photographer

I love taking pictures and sharing pictures. Memories, faces and moments are captured in pictures that become treasures. One of my dearest friends, Heather, was gracious enough to take wonderful pictures for us at our very first SerenDIPity in 2010. She captures beautiful photographs with love and joy. Many of our special memories as a family have been caught lovingly on camera by Heather.

However, Heather and her husband, Rob, were our guests. And although she would be glad to take pictures as she dips the evening away with Rob, we wanted them to enjoy SerenDIPity together and without the accessory of a camera hanging from their arms!

So the following year and the years since, we have hired photographers. We were delighted to know that both candid and posed shots were being taken all night. We were able to enjoy the pictures later and share them with our friends. Again, the ability to hire a photographer enhances your experience and your guests' as well.

Considering your budget boundaries, a student photographer can be hired. This is someone who is learning the craft of photography and welcomes opportunities to use their talents and sharpen their skills. Student photographers are affordable and usually very delighted to have the opportunity.

The last few years we have hired a lovely student photographer named Toni. We shared with her what kinds of pictures we would like to have, and she added her own flair and vision as well. We are blessed.

You may want to have one of your older children, or a niece, nephew or neighborhood student to take pictures. Whatever fits your budget and likes, be sure to have pictures to remember SerenDIPity!

To contact our photographers, Heather, Meg and Toni, please turn to the notes portion at the end of this book. Their contact information is listed and they would love to hear from you!

Shopping For Party Items

Usually about six weeks before SerenDIPity, I begin shopping. Remember, I tend to work ahead. If this is too early for you, then adjust your time frame and work at your own best pace. Some people are wired to work better under pressure. I admire you! On the other hand, if you want to do shopping even sooner than I recommend, I applaud you!

Panache and Preparation

If I have a color theme for the party, I look for affordable paper products that coordinate with my theme. Wholesale stores, overstock stores and discount party stores are great resources. Plan on each guest using a few plates and cups each. I also purchase plastic spoons and forks for the dipping and eating festivities.

If you decide to have favors, gifts or prizes, keep your eye out for appropriate items at stores like Home Goods or Marshall's or even dollar stores. Our prizes are usually culinary or hostess items that the winner can use again when they entertain or when simply serving a family meal.

Getting Your Recipes Together

If you haven't done so already, you will want to gather your thoughts and recipes about four weeks before SerenDIPity. Whether you create your own dip or use a recipe you found in a book or online, having everything organized and together will help you as SerenDIPity gets closer. We usually serve four dips (not eligible for prizes) ~ two savory and two sweet.

Write down the names of your recipes and the ingredients you will eventually need to purchase. If you want to have a special presentation for your dip, gather props or serving dishes that you want to use. Your excitement will heighten as your creative and culinary juices flow in preparation.

Wrap Gifts/Prizes/Party Favors

If you are awarding prizes or giving party favors, wrap them up to two weeks ahead of time. Keep a list of the prizes you are awarding and tag each one appropriately. This can be a time-consuming task, so having it done ahead of time will bring great relief to you later as the SerenDIPity approaches.

Prizes wrapped, tagged and ready to go!

Gather Serving Utensils, Bowls, Baskets and Electric Cords

A week before your SerenDIPity, gather together any serving items you will use and those you will make available to your guests (if they forget theirs or need to borrow yours). This way, when your utensil-borrowing guests arrive, they can get what they need from you or your hostess assistant. I also am sure to have extra toothpicks and wooden skewers available as well. We keep a stock of tea light candles in case anyone has a serving tray kept warm by tea lights.

Electrical Hook Up

Being the electrical engineer that he is, Jim takes charge (get it?) of electrical set ups for hot dips. Guests bringing and serving hot dips will need to plug in and often need to borrow an extension cord. We prepare our kitchen buffet counter exclusively to accommodate guests with hot dips since we have wall outlets available and Jim can run extension cords.

Warm Spicy Maryland Crab Dip brought by my friends, Tom and Jen, in 2011. Our guests loved it and it won an award at SerenDIPity that year! This was on our "hot counter" in the kitchen where Jim had electrical hook-ups ready to go!
(Photo by Megan Brock)
http://allrecipes.com/Recipe/Spicy-Maryland-Crab-Dip/Detail.aspx

Grocery Shopping

Keep a running list of grocery items you will need including beverages and your ingredients needed for the dips you are serving. Shop a day or two before, but be sure perishable items are fresh for your guests (such as fruit and vegetables). We also purchase plenty of aluminum foil, plastic wrap and some new disposable containers with lids so our guests can package up any leftovers and bring them home easily. You'll want to pick up toothpicks, small wooden skewers and place cards (to be placed next to the guest's dip with the name and competition number of the dip).

Prepare Your Own Dips

If possible (and sometimes the recipe recommends it for best flavor), prepare your dips the day before. This will afford you more time the day of for finishing touches on house cleaning and party set up. Have whatever you will need to serve your dips at the ready. Label your dips on place cards with the name of the dip for your guests. (We do not include our dips in the competition, so our dips are not assigned a number. See Chapter 6 for more about this.)

Clean Out The Refrigerator and Clean The House

Be sure to clean out and wash up your refrigerator as best as possible. You will need room for your ingredients and dips, and some of your guests will need refrigerator space as well. Clean out frig doors and drawers. You may also want to make extra room in your freezer if you are planning on stocking up on ice cubes for the party.

If you are able to have someone assist you in cleaning (young, energetic students wanting to earn some money are a great resource for this!), schedule them to come the day before or the morning of SerenDIPity. If you are cleaning yourself, pace yourself so you don't become overwhelmed and discouraged. While you want a clean and tidy home for your guests, they aren't going to notice the things to which you weren't able to tend. Truth is, your floors will need to be cleaned the next day anyway!

Check to be sure soft soap containers are filled in every bathroom, toilet paper rolls are available for refilling, hand towels and hostess paper towels are available and that candles are placed and ready to be lit.

Choose The Better Part ~ Take Time To Sit and Pray

At the Home of Martha and Mary

"As Jesus and His disciples were on their way, He came to a village where a woman named Martha opened her home to Him. She had a sister called Mary, who sat at the Lord's feet listening to what He said. But Martha was distracted by all the preparations that had to be made. She came to Him and asked, 'Lord, don't You care that my sister has left me to do the work by myself? Tell her to help me!' 'Martha, Martha,' the Lord answered, "you are worried and upset about many things, but few things are needed—or indeed only one. Mary has chosen what is better, and it will not be taken away from her."
~ Luke 10:38-42

The morning of SerenDIPity, have your devotional time. Don't skip it. Open His Word, dip deep in and ask Him to minister to you. I hope that every morning your quiet time with the Lord is extra-special for you, and especially as you open your home in hospitality to your guests for SerenDIPity.

Before your guests arrive, be sure to leave plenty of time to ready yourself and to pray. If you are married, take a few minutes to pray together with your spouse and with your children. Ask the Lord's continued blessing in your home and for His sweet presence to bless the fellowship at your SerenDIPity. You never know, you may be entertaining angels without knowing it. *"Do **not forget to** show hospitality to strangers, for by so doing some people have shown hospitality to angels without knowing it." – Hebrews 13:2*

Chapter 4

Invitations ~ Setting The Stage

"What a day of surprises it has been!...The ineffable glory of Jesus' Saviorhood lies in the fact that He is always able to do exceedingly abundantly all that we ask or think."

~ F. Boreham (Boulevard of Paradise ~ "A Day of Surprises")

"I have invited guests..." ~ 1 Samuel 9:24

Invitations are especially sacred and meaningful to me. In Chapter One, I shared with you an invitation that changed my life forever. Literally. Receiving Christ as my Savior and Lord is the foundation, anchor and purpose of my life. His hand on my life and His breath into my being are why I rise each day. Life without Him would be empty and meaningless to me. His redeeming invitation to me has changed my life and is daily changing my heart. If you would like, take a moment and read The Table Testimony (http://histablefortwo.blogspot.com/p/table-testimony.html). He has a table prepared for you. He wants to fill you at His table. ***"You shall be filled at My table..." Ezekiel 39:20*** The Lord of Hosts beckons us to come to His wedding banquet. As we unfold and accept His invitation, we are seated at the table of the King.

I am devoting this entire chapter to invitations because I love invitations in every sense of the word. The intangible and tangible blessings of invitations are of great value to our hearts. An invitation speaks of acceptance, inclusion, care, love, worth and friendship. When we receive an invitation to a gathering, we are so blessed and humbled to be included. In a sense, the invitation says *"You are important to us"*.

Your invitation to your SerenDIPity party will be the knock on the door of your guest's heart to come and share food, faith and fellowship with you. SerenDIPity is about surprisability! Your guests will be DIPlighted to receive your invitation. Even if they are unable to attend, the fact that you reached out and extended the invitation to join you will be a delight to their hearts. I encourage you to take extra care as you prepare your invitation, whether they are cyber invitations or paper invitations. Both extending and receiving invitations are an honor.

Guest Lists

Creating guests lists can be difficult and tedious. It is impossible to invite everyone. You want your guests to be blessed, and yet you don't want to hurt the hearts of those who are not on your guest list. We have all experienced that *"I wasn't invited"* feeling. And it stinks. As adults we understand that not everyone is invited to everything. But there is still that prick in our hearts that happens when we hear of a social affair to which we were not invited that we would really enjoy attending or to which many of our friends were invited.

So as you begin putting together your guest list for SerenDIPity, pray for God's leading and for Him to gather together the guests for your event. As a woman who enjoys entertaining and gathering people together for fellowship, guest lists to me have become an offering to the Lord.

Godly Guest List Etiquette

I believe Luke 14 teaches us godly guest list etiquette. God's Word tells us to extend invitations to unassuming guests. Jesus says to look beyond the obvious guests on our lists, such as treasured family and close friends, and to reach out to the downtrodden as well. Invite guests who perhaps cannot repay you with a return invitation. Your reward will be at the "resurrection of the righteous". *"Then Jesus said to His host, 'When you give a luncheon or dinner, do not invite your friends, your brothers or relatives, or your rich neighbors…But when you give a banquet, invite the poor, the crippled, the lame, the blind, and you will be blessed. Although they cannot repay you, you will be repaid at the resurrection of the righteous.'" Luke 14:12-14 (NIV)*

When my husband, children and I make our party guest lists together (for adult parties or children parties), we prayerfully ask the Lord to put those on our hearts who would be blessed by receiving an invitation. Perhaps a friend who is not financially able to host birthday parties themselves. Or someone who is dealing with paralyzing emotional pain or in the midst of a depressive episode. Maybe someone who is going through a painful season of life. Perhaps a friend who is shy and tends to be socially isolated. Or the one who has rough edges, is not easy to be around and doesn't see God's loving acceptance. The poor, the lame, the crippled and the blind. All of us need to be encouraged to fellowship and to not isolate ourselves.

Truth is, without Jesus and His redemptive love, we are all "the poor, the crippled, the lame, the blind." Even in Christian circles, we can feel like the outcast or the unwanted guest. Just as we are chosen by God to be guests of honor at His party, let's invite unlikely guests and place them at the top of our own guest lists. You are honoring God by inviting the poor, lame, crippled and blind. *"He who oppresses the poor shows contempt for their Maker, but whoever is kind to the needy honors God" (Proverbs 14:31, NIV).* And by extending an invitation as unto the Lord, we receive the intrinsic joy of honoring God as we honor others with an invitation.

Invitations

I have a confession to make. I am a stationery addict! And I don't want to receive intervention!

Since I was a very young girl I have loved note cards, writing paper and invitations. Collecting stationery of every kind was a passionate hobby of mine growing up. Still today I love having a plethora of note cards on hand to send to family and friends. My favorite stores to visit and browse through are card shops and unique stationery boutiques. Enjoying the look and texture of stationery is a pleasure for my heart and senses. Call me nerdy.

So while I appreciate the efficiency and technological savvy of online invitations, I am nostalgic for paper invitations!

Let's chat about the benefits of both online and traditional paper invitations. Because I am partial to traditional paper invitations, I ask for your grace to let me begin there as I shamelessly display a little sentimental favoritism.

Paper Invitations

Imagine your family and friends opening their mailbox and seeing a festive envelope with a first-class stamp on it! It will be the first piece of mail they open. The advertisements and bills will be pushed to the side, and your invitation will be the opening act of that day's daily mail.

This is where the excitement of SerenDIPity begins!

Invitations reflect your personality and your hospitality style. Do not rush in picking an invitation. You can be keeping a lookout for invitations in the weeks before mailing them for just the perfect style.

Invitations ~ Setting the Stage

Your unique invitation will set the tone and state the theme for your SerenDIPity. Your invitations can be simple or exquisite, understated or extravagant.

Keeping your entertainment budget in mind, check clearance racks of your local card stores and gift shops. They often have printable paper invitations on sale. Even dollar stores have cute invitations and printable letterhead that you can use to create an invitation. I often check www.dayspring.com for their clearance sales on stationery. I buy when suitable items are on sale and then keep them in storage until I need them. http://www.dayspring.com/sale_and_clearance/ Invitations do not need to be expensive. Rather, you can create something that will bless your guests as they open them and read the details of your SerenDIPity.

If you have the room in your budget, you can create paper invitations online and even include photographs if you would like. Often you can search for coupon codes or take advantage of sale promotions on stationery sites. These sites will frequently offer free shipping and up to 30% off orders. Here are just a few sites that I have used with discounts and promotions:

www.simplytoimpress.com

www.tinyprints.com

www.vistaprint.com

www.shutterfly.com

Because we have hosted SerenDIPity for several years now, I have a wonderful collection of pictures of our guests and their savory and sweet dips. For the last few years, I have created paper invitations online using pictures of the previous year's dips.

Again, your invitations can be simple or creative, inexpensive to more costly. Just be sure they reflect your personality and your style as they set the stage for your SerenDIPity!

SerenDIPity: Celebrating Dips, Faith & Friendship

"A desire fulfilled is sweet to the soul…"

~ Proverbs 13:19 (ESV)

Online Cyber Invitations

Though I am a fan of paper invitations, there are indeed many benefits to cyber invitations:

- Most invitations are free of charge
- You incur no postage expenses
- You benefit from the efficiency of sending the invitation immediately (especially if you are running behind in getting your invitations out)
- Your guests can RSVP online, which is convenient for them and easy for you to keep track of responses
- You can send messages to your guests with any updated information with the click of a button
- You can create the invitations using pre-made templates
- You control your invitation options (such as keeping the guest list private or making it visible and public to all guests)

Many online invitation sites are available. Here are a few I have used myself or from which I have received invitations.

www.signupgenius.com

www.punchbowl.com

www.smilebox.com

www.evite.com

www.ejovo.com

Online invitations are appealing to hosts and hostesses. And with so many creative sites in cyber world today, they are all great resources!

Invitations ~ Setting the Stage

What to Include On Your Invitation

Whether you choose paper or cyber invitations for SerenDIPity, there is some pertinent information you want to include for your guests. You want to be sure they are prepared and "in the know". This will make them feel more comfortable attending and excited about the celebration.

In your invitation envelope, you may want to include:

- Invitation (date, time, place, RSVP deadline, directions, contact information)
- Recipe Card (ask each guest to bring their recipe with them)
- Ticket for a Grand Prize (if applicable)
- Invitation Insert (if necessary)

Recipe Card

(Photo by Megan Brock)

SerenDIPity: Celebrating Dips, Faith & Friendship

At our first SerenDIPity, some of our guests were so thoughtful and brought their recipe written out on a recipe card to share with us and the other guests. I loved this idea and began including recipe cards in our invitations ever since. We ask each guest to bring their recipe written out on the recipe card. These can be displayed with the dip because many guests want to share and receive new recipes. Also, I keep the recipe cards each year in recipe books and they serve as a wonderful hospitality resource for me and our guests!

Invitation Insert

If you can't (or don't want to) fit all of your information on the actual paper invitation, it is a good idea to include a separate, pretty piece of paper with your additional details. If you are choosing a cyber-invitation, there is usually a place where you can write comments or notes for your guests.

Here is the wording from the insert we included in our SerenDIPity 2013 invitation. This will give you a good flavor of what you might want to include. Also, I feel it very important to give credit where credit is due. I hope to reflect that in my life in general and also through written and spoken words. So if it wasn't my idea to being with, I always try to credit the person from whom I received the idea or inspiration. ***"I am looking for what may be credited to you…" ~ Philippians 4:17***

Our 2013 Invitation Insert

We hope you can join us for our annual SerenDIPity!

Saturday, March 16, 2013, at 6:30 pm

The Sloan Home, [Home address], {City, State, Zip]
Kindly rsvp by 3/8, [phone number] or [email]

Invitations ~ Setting the Stage

Bring one DIP – either an appetizer (savory) or dessert (sweet)!

Prizes in each category (savory and sweet) will be awarded for Tastiest, Most Original,

Best Presentation (originally inspired by Erika) and more!

Prizes will also be awarded for Warm Dips.

The Cutest Shoes prize will be awarded by Sharon.

Jim will award "Manly Dip" prizes (category originally inspired by Mike & Lynne).

Other Awards: Best Shoes for Men (inspired by Tim & Steven)

Couples Award (both in a couple prepare a dip ~ inspired by Geoff & Jennifer and continued by Rob & Heather)

Best Purchased Dip (for those with the heart to make a dip but not the time)

We will be serving (not eligible for a prize):

Grilled Steak and Chicken Strips with Chimichurri Dip

Warm Turnip Green Dip with French Bread (recipe by my friend Lysa)

Mississippi Sin Dip with Italian Toasts (recipe by my friend Zoe)

Raspberry Coconut Cream Dip with Assorted Sweets

Each guest will receive a parting gift/favor.

"Therefore you will give parting gifts…" Micah 1:14

Please bring the enclosed recipe card with your recipe on it.

"Eat what is good, and you will delight in the richest of fare." Isaiah 55:2

SerenDIPity: Celebrating Dips, Faith & Friendship

Thanks and Kudos – "I am looking for what may be credited to you…" (Phil. 4:17)

Sincere thanks to Karen who enthusiastically and beautifully addressed the invitation envelopes.

"A letter will tell you much; but the envelope will often tell you more." – Frank Boreham

Dips pictured from last year's SerenDIPity appearing on this year's invitation and envelope labels were by: Erika, Cheryl, Lucille, Lynne, Ronna, Jen,

Kristin, Deb and Lynn. Thank you!

Pictures taken by Toni Valentini. https://www.facbook.com/nowpicturethis

Looking forward to DIPping the evening away with you!

DIPlighted by your friendship, Jim & Sharon

Of course, you will tailor your information to your celebration. You want your guests to know they are warmly invited, and you want them to be up to date with any details you can share so they feel at ease and prepared.

Envelopes

"A letter will tell you much; but the envelope will often tell you more."
~ Frank Boreham

Snazz up your invitation envelopes if you can. It will be the fun first impression on your guest when they receive the invitation in the mail. Use colorful ink and pretty stamps. Add a tasteful sticker or two. My gracious friend, Karen, offered to calligraphy all of our envelopes for our most recent SerenDIPity. She was so excited to do them, and they were beautiful! I supplied her with the envelopes, purple Sharpie fine-point markers and all of the addresses. She literally was done them in under an hour and so many guests commented on how exceptional they were!

Remember your invitation, in whatever form, is the knock on the door to your guests' hearts to come and fellowship, enjoy delicious food, fun-loving competition, meaningful conversation and hearty laughter. Make your invitations and envelopes unique and special.

Chapter 5
Prizes and Pleasant Surprises!

"Expect the unexpected! God leads us to places where His power shows up in new and astonishing ways. May an awesome display of His power strengthen your faith."

~ Priscilla Shirer (One In A Million Bible Study)

Prizes from SerenDIPity 2011
(Photo by Megan Brock)

The friendly and fun-loving competition that has been so much fun for our guests has been a personally serendipitous part of SerenDIPity for me. I mentioned earlier that I am not a competitor by nature. I am more of a cheerleader – cheering others on and encouraging them to use their God-given gifts to run their unique race well.

Ironically, awarding prizes for SerenDIPity was borne solely out of my love for giving rather than an appreciation of or interest in competition. Wanting to give guests awards for their creativity and labors of love, and knowing that gifts are great rewards and motivators, prizes for the guests have been a fabulous element of SerenDIPity since its inception!

Our prizes themselves often include culinary-esque items such as unique serving dishes and bowls, pretty serving utensils, cook books, measuring spoons, aprons, kitchen towels, flavored olive oils, quick pre-packaged dip mixes, cupcake papers and decorations, recipe cards, culinary-related note cards and small gift certificates to fun places to eat or grab dessert, such as ice cream.

Prizes and Pleasant Surprises!

This is a great example of a creative presentation.

Our neighbors, Michael and Lynn, brought delicious lamb meatballs with a Cilantro Raita dip to SerenDIPity 2013. Their inspiring presentation looked like a sheep pasture. Loved it!

(Photo by Toni Valentini)

Another veggie attractive display was brought by my friend Tammie.
Her vegetable display won a prize!
She would want you to know her father helped her.
I want you to know she creates amazing cupcake art!

(Photo by Megan Brock)

Prizes and Pleasant Surprises!

This Turtle Cheesecake Dip makes my mouth water just looking at the picture!
My dear friend Shannon brought this to SerenDIPity 2012.
The dip itself made a spectacular presentation! Not to mention it was delicious!
You can find the recipe here: http://www.cdkitchen.com/recipes

(Photo by Toni Valentini)

Here are the categories of awards we have given. You may want to keep it to just a few or perhaps add your own! (Let me know what great ideas you have!) We have similar awards for savory (appetizer) dips, sweet (dessert) dips and warm dips. (Note: warm dips can be either savory or sweet.)

1. Savory – Tastiest
2. Savory – Most Original
3. Savory – Best Presentation
4. Sweet – Tastiest
5. Sweet – Most Original
6. Sweet – Best Presentation
7. Warm Dips – Tastiest
8. Warm Dips—Most Original
9. Warm Dips – Best Presentation
10. Manly Dips (Jim's favorite category) – Tastiest
11. Manly Dips – Most Original
12. Manly Dips – Best Presentation
13. Couple Awards – (when both the husband and wife prepare a dip and bring them)
14. Cutest Shoes (women)
15. Best Manly Shoes (men…since our manly guys put themselves in the running!)
16. Tastiest Store-Bought Dip – (for those with the heart to bring a dip but not the time to prepare it)
17. Secret Surprise Awards (have a few little extra things on hand for some surprises…whatever moves you!)
18. Grand Prize

If The Shoe Fits

As I mentioned earlier, having a prize for cute shoes was an unexpected surprise from our first SerenDIPity. Our always-stylish hostess assistant, Jill, wore fabulous animal print high heel shoes

Prizes and Pleasant Surprises!

that wonderfully took center stage for shoe enthusiasts like myself. Other shoe enthusiasts and I took note of some great pairs of shoes as we dipped our way through the evening. Because surprisability is a necessary ingredient in SerenDIPity, I am always looking for ways to surprise guests. That night I surprised guests who were wearing extraordinarily cute shoes. Since then, we have made it a whimsical part of our SerenDIPity. My dear friend, Maria, is well known for wearing show-stopping shoes, and she has won a few prizes in the shoe category herself!

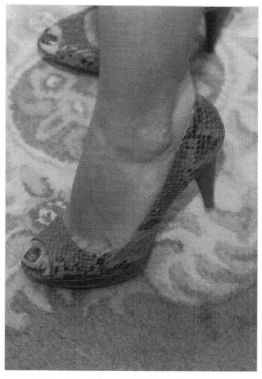

Maria's shoes ~ SerenDIPity 2011

(Photo by Megan Brock)

Here are Maria and her husband, Tito, at SerenDIPity 2013. We may just have to consider having a bow tie prize next year. They took the dress code of "Smart Casual" to a new level.
(Photo by Toni Valentini)

When we stated in our invitation for SerenDIPity 2011 that we would be having a prize for "Cutest Shoes", never did we realize that two of the winners would be men!! Two of my girlfriends' husbands, who happen to be fashion savvy in the manliest sense, wore great manly shoes and took home prizes – much to our surprise! Surprisability!!! For the guests….and the host and hostess!

Prizes and Pleasant Surprises!

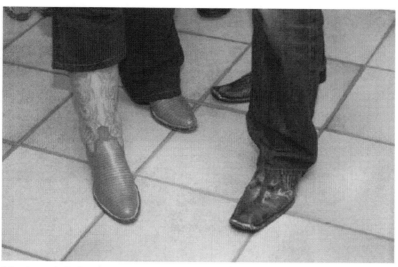

Manly stylish footwear by my girlfriends' husbands!! ~ Tim and Steven ~ SerenDIPity 2011
(Photo by Megan Brock)

Maybe you couldn't care less about footwear for men and women! This is just an unexpected little part we have added to our SerenDIPity after some of our guests wore some fabulous shoes. Your SerenDIPity will reflect you as host and hostess. Be on the lookout for things that excite you and be prepared to surprise your guests!

> *"Though I have walked with God for several decades, I must confess I still find much about Him incomprehensible and mysterious. But this much I know: He delights in surprising us. He dots our pilgrimage from earth to heaven with amazing serendipities..."*
>
> *~ Charles R. Swindoll*

Comfy shoes worn by our friends Troy, Mary Beth and Erika at SerenDIPity 2013.

We love that our guests sport their own style and express themselves comfortably!

(Photo by Toni Valentini)

A Splash of Surprisability

At SerenDIPity 2012, we didn't tell our guests that we would be on the lookout for a guest who had a scripture displayed with their dip. But at the end of the evening, we surprised the one guest who had a scripture with her beautifully-displayed dip.

Prizes and Pleasant Surprises!

SerenDIPity 2012 (Photo by Toni Valentini)

And what was her prize? Something very appropriate – a SerenDIPity Bible!

SerenDIPity 2012 (Photo by Toni Valentini)

One year we gave a little prize to the person with the most unique RSVP. Another year we gave a prize the day after SerenDIPity just to keep the fun going. Think of interesting ways you can surprise your guests before, during and after SerenDIPity!

Grand Prize

We have had the blessing of giving away a Grand Prize to one of our guests the last few years. I have made either a silver or golden ticket and included it in each invitation envelope with the last name of the guest written on the back. The guests bring their ticket to SerenDIPity and give it to our hostess assistance when they arrive. She puts all the tickets in a hat box. At the end of the evening, after all of the prizes are awarded, one of our children picks one of the Grand Prize tickets and announces the winner. It really is a lot of fun!

I am honored to have as one of my very dearest friends the fabulously talented Lucille Osborn. Lucille is a Professional Food Stylist who has worked with several well-known chefs and cookbook authors, such as Ina Garten, Mary Ann Esposito and Judy Rosenberg. Lucille has worked on such television shows as Home Matters and Epicurious. Most recently she has been a food stylist in the QVC broadcast kitchens right here in Pennsylvania.

Several years ago, Lucille asked me to join her and a few other friends for an intimate lunch at one of our favorite girlfriend cafes in the area. She wanted to share her God-breathed inspiration of how she could use her God-given gifts, talents, skill and experience to serve the Lord. From that lunch, her ministry Psalm 34:8 Cooking was launched. A gifted teacher, Lucille combines her passion for culinary arts and her reverence for God's Word. She teaches life-changing truths from Scripture along with a cooking class all at the same time.

Hosting intimate classes to large conferences, Lucille's menu of classes include titles such as "Breakfast By The Sea", "Bread of Life",

Prizes and Pleasant Surprises!

"A Broken Life Transformed", "Feeding The Multitudes", "Salt of The Earth" and "I Am The True Vine".

As a blessing to our guests and also to Lucille as she diligently serves the Lord in this unique ministry, Jim and I have been privileged to give away a Grand Prize at SerenDIPity of an intimate Psalm 34:8 Cooking Class for ten to our winner. Excitement builds throughout the evening until our Grand Prize winner of SerenDIPity is chosen.

Your Grand Prize could be anything from offering to host a SerenDIPity for children of your guests, or having another couple or family for a Sunday dinner, or preparing an afternoon picnic in the park for friends. Use your creativity and think of things that will bring people together and refresh them. Your Grand Prize will reflect the hospitality heart of SerenDIPity.

The SerenDIPity Voting Ballot

Whether you decide to include prizes as part of your SerenDIPity, or just to have a friendly competition without prizes, you will need to have a voting ballot for each of your guests. Be sure to have plenty of sharpened pencils ready too!

SerenDIPity: Celebrating Dips, Faith & Friendship

The voting ballots can remain anonymous and guests do not need to put their names. In addition to our prize categories, we include a place at the bottom for comments. Guests may write suggestions for next year or simply just leave a note about a dip or detail of SerenDIPity they especially enjoyed. Make your voting ballot your own style and personality.

I print our voting ballots on card stock and always have extra ready. Have a place for your guests to return the voting ballots so your hostess assistant can tally them up.

Here is our voting ballot from SerenDIPity 2013:

Prizes and Pleasant Surprises!

SerenDIPity 2013 ~ Voting Ballot

Appetizers – "Savory"

Tastiest Dip: #_____   Name of Dip: _____

Most Original Dip: #_____   Name of Dip: _____

Best Presentation: #_____   Name of Dip: _____

Best Warm Dip: #_____   Name of Dip: _____

Best "Man Dip" # _____   Name of Dip: _____

Desserts – "Sweet"

Tastiest Dip: #_____   Name of Dip: _____

Most Original Dip: #_____   Name of Dip: _____

Best Presentation: #_____   Name of Dip: _____

Best Store-Bought Dip: #_____   Name of Dip: _____

SerenDIPitous Comments and/or SerenDIPitous Write-In Vote:

Two of our SerenDIPity enthusiasts, Kenny and Lilo, suggested we start doing online voting at SerenDIPity! This is a great idea and would save time in calculating votes by hand. While we may entertain this idea and come up with an easy program to record votes during the party on our laptops, for now we enjoy the old-fashioned way of voting…with paper and pencil.

Chapter 6

Only One Rule ~ No Double Dipping!

*"Give me neither poverty nor riches;
feed me with the food that is needful for me..."*

~ Proverbs 30:8

The preparation of SerenDIPity has been completed. You have budgeted, planned, sent invitations, shopped, wrapped prizes and printed voting ballots. Your own dips are made and ready to be displayed and served. Your home is cleaned and the door is wide open. You are showered and dressed. Your dog has been to the groomer. You've refilled the liquid hand soaps in the bathrooms. Your candles are lit, and you are ready to receive your guests.

Much of your planning and preparation has been joyful and fun. Inevitably, however, there has been some stress. This is not unusual with entertaining, so I want to give you some tips and insights we have gleaned after hosting several SerenDIPities. This chapter is a pot luck of things to consider before, during and after hosting a SerenDIPity.

Sit back and get a cup of coffee, a glass of lemonade or an iced tea. Relax and take a deep breath. Everything is going to be fine. This section may be your favorite of the entire book!

Desserts Spelled Backwards is "Stressed"!

"A feast is made for laughter…"

~ Ecclesiastes 10:19

My sweet and refreshingly honest girlfriend confided in me after she attended her first SerenDIPity. And though she was light-heartedly laughing when she shared her heart with me, I listened intently and with surprise at what she was saying. *"I was so nervous when I came to my first SerenDIPity. I wondered how my dip would compare with others. I wasn't sure exactly what to expect. I was a little stressed out about it."*

My initial response was a little chuckle, not imagining that she actually felt this way. This girlfriend is smart, beautiful, talented and confident. But realizing she was serious as she opened up with tender vulnerability, I think my jaw dropped to the ground in astonishment. *She had been nervous about coming to SerenDIPity.* Wow! I had not considered that. I was so thankful for her sharing her heart with me. Her truth and candor changed the way I open my home in hospitality for SerenDIPity and how I entertain company.

Stressed out?

Nervous?

These were NOT some of the pre-festivity emotions I wanted any of my friends and guests to be feeling! I knew the stress the host and hostess could feel, but my girlfriend's words reminded me to be caring and sensitive to the possible stress guests were feeling.

Because being competitive isn't part of my nature, it is not important for me personally if I win something. I'd actually prefer others to win. It makes me happy. Yes, if I am playing on a team, then I do my best to contribute to help the team achieve their goal (which is usually to win). So while I want to work at something with all of my heart as unto the Lord, my personal goal is not usually to win. *"Whatever you do, work at it with all your heart, as working for the Lord, not for human masters, since you know that you will receive an inheritance from the Lord as a reward. It is the Lord Christ you are serving." Colossians 3:23-24*

The light-hearted competition of SerenDIPity was more about giving prizes than about serious competition. That's what it was for me anyway. But for people who are competitive by nature, who want to win and who enjoy the challenge of healthy competition, their perspective is completely different. My wonderfully competitive girlfriend's candor opened my eyes and heart to this truth. And she has made me a better hostess by sharing her heart.

God has blessed us with many friends who are indeed competitive, who are talented athletically and who enjoy pushing the limits and being challenged. Translate all of that into a SerenDIPity that awards prizes for the best dips in a variety of categories, and we have some exuberant and high-spirited participants!

We also may have some nervousness.

I also then considered friends who may not get out much due to being in a difficult season of life with demands and priorities at home. For those guests, it may have taken some Pentagon-level planning for them to get away from home for a few hours to attend SerenDIPity. I don't take it lightly that they have carved out the time to come, so I want them to feel refreshed.

Add to that guests who have a little social anxiety to begin with, or those that may be somewhat introverted, and you begin to admire the courage it takes for them to come to get out and socialize. As the hostess, I want to make all of our guests feel as welcomed and as comfortable as possible. This gives the guests "freedom to move about the cabin" a bit and enjoy the camaraderie of fellowship. Bathing the gathering in prayer, my husband and I are sure to ask for the Lord's blessing and favor upon the evening. God is faithful to bring serendipitous and tasty fruit as we make the time to be together.

After the guests have all arrived and before we start the dipping festivities, Jim opens in prayer to set the tone for the evening and to invite Jesus to be present with us. We pray that He receives our conversation and fellowship with each other as acts of worship. We ask Him to fill our home with peace, love and joy. We thank Him for how we are blessed and humbled by the friendships He has given us.

Thoughtfully go through your list of all of those attending your SerenDIPity. Pray for each one individually and for each couple. Ask the Lord to give you a sensitive heart toward anyone who may need some extra encouragement as they step out and accept your invitation of hospitality.

Be on the lookout for God's miraculous surprise blessings!

"In each situation, hope seemed futile. Yet God used every one of these circumstances to bring Himself glory while allowing the participants a miraculous glimpse of His awesome power. If you can't figure out how to navigate the path before you, take heart. When you can't imagine that Divine intervention is at your doorstep, get ready. Doing life God's way, especially when times seem difficult, often includes miraculous surprises."

~ Priscilla Shirer (One In A Million Bible Study)

The Lay of the Land ~ Dip Staging Areas

For ease of displaying and serving your dips, and for the necessity of motivating your guests to move around your house a bit (instead of all congregating in the kitchen), you will want to have "staging areas" for your various dips. Your guests will know where to find the savory dips, the hot dips, the manly dips and the sweet dips. They can move around tasting the various dips and enjoy conversation at the same time.

So for instance, here is our current set-up for the various dips at SerenDIPity:

- Savory Dips – Dining room table and (and living room bench table if necessary)
- Hot Dips – Kitchen buffet counter (near electrical outlets)
- Manly Dips – Finished basement (with large leather sectional and big screen TV, booth table and refreshment bar
- Sweet Dips – Kitchen table

You may choose to mix things up a bit and put your dips all around rather than organizing them in like categories on various tables. However, we have found this works best for our guests, and it is very easy when it comes time to fill out the voting ballots.

Check-In Sheets, Assigned Numbers and Place Cards

When our guests arrive, our Hostess Assistants are ready to greet them in the foyer. One of the assistants takes their jackets while Jill gets details about their dip. Keeping simple lists on columned paper, she registers the dips under four categories -- savory (appetizer), hot, manly and sweet (dessert). Below are some sample check-in sheets from our SerenDIPity.

Savory Dips (Appetizers)

Number	Name of Dip	Guest
A-1	Buffalo Chicken Dip	Eric and Rita
A-2	Campanata Dip	Paul and Heather
A-3	Jalapeno Pepper Spread	Jerry and Robin
A-4	Redneck Caviar	Bob and Kim
A-5	Gazpacho Salsa	Craig and Jody
A-6	Goat Cheese & Pistachio Dip	Ramon and Pamela
A-7	Brie en Croute	Corinna

Sweet Dips (Desserts)

Number	Name of Dip	Guest
D-1	Rainbow Cheesecake Dip	Brian and Adina
D-2	Mousse Carpon Dip	Mark and Laurie
D-3	Cookie Dough Dip	Andrea and Shannon
D-4	Chocolate Dipped Bacon	Bill and Cyndee

Hot Dips

Number	Name of Dip	Guest
H-1	Butterscotch Dip	Jim and Kathy
H-2	Hot Corn Dip	Mary
H-3	Charleston Cheese Dip	Kelley and Nancy
H-4	Corned Beef and Swiss Dip	John and Kim

Manly Dips

Number	Name of Dip	Guest
M-1	Guaca-manly	Geoff and Jenn
M-2	Cowboys and Onions	Tim and Kathy
M-3	Carnesita	Tito and Maria
M-4	Caprese Pizza Dip	Steve and Kim

Once the dips are recorded and a place card is made for them, they can be displayed in the appropriate area.

Only One Rule ~ No Double Dipping!

SerenDIPity 2011 by my friend Cathi (Photo by Megan Brock)

(Important note: we keep all dip makers ANONYMOUS until the end of the evening after prizes are awarded. It is more fun, mysterious and suspenseful that way!)

Be sure to give your guests plenty of time to eat and enjoy all of the dips at a relaxed pace. After a couple of hours, ask them to fill out and return their voting ballots to your Hostess Assistant, who will then tally up the votes for you. During the vote counting and the awards part of the evening, your guests will continue to enjoy noshing on the dips and going back to the ones they liked the most.

Leftovers

"...send portions of food and to celebrate with great joy..."
~ Nehemiah 8:12

Inevitably, your guests will have leftovers of their dips and dippers. Be sure to have plenty of disposable storage containers (such as GladWare or Ziploc), plastic wrap and aluminum foil available for them to pack up at the end of the evening. You and your hostess assistants can help with this. Your guests will appreciate you thinking of this end-of-party detail.

Parting Gifts ~ Party Favors

"Therefore you will give parting gifts…"
~ Micah 1:14

Every one of our guests put so much thought and time into preparing their dip for SerenDIPity, often including financial resources (can you say "ingredients for seafood dip"??). I like each guest to go home with a little something to remember the evening by and to say thank you to them for making SerenDIPity so special. You can make something homemade or find inexpensive culinary-related party favors in stores and online. Everyone (especially the women!) enjoy taking a favor home. I wish everyone could win a prize, but the favors go a long way in saying thank you.

"I will make savory food…"
~ Genesis 27:9 (NKJV)

Only One Rule ~ No Double Dipping!

This beautifully-presented Tzatziki Dip was made by my dear friend Lucille for SerenDIPity 2012.

Her food is delicious and beautiful ~ art a la carte! Visit Lucille here ~ www.psalm348cooking.com

(Photo by Toni Valentini)

Chapter 7

Savory Spoonfuls

I wish I could share all of the dips that our guests have brought over the years. Truly, they are very impressive and inspired! I would love to introduce you to each guest and their culinary handiwork. As I have said before, our family and friends have made SerenDIPity what it is. They have raised the bar and keep the fun and spirited competition going every year.

Just a few of the award-winning savory dip recipes are shared in this chapter. But more will be shared online at www.serendipitydipsbook.com and https://www.facbook.com/SerendipityCelebratingDipsFaithFriendships.

SerenDIPity: Celebrating Dips, Faith & Friendship

Savory Appetizer Dip Recipes

Crab Mousse Dip

SerenDIPity 2011 (Photo by Megan Brock)

It makes complete sense that my friend Kathy's dip that won in the savory category is a recipe handed down to her from her mother-in-love, Donna. Kathy is a one-of-a-kind wife and mom to her husband, Tim, and her four boys. Kathy's love for her family is evident in her everyday life. She serves as such an example and mentor to other Christian women by her sincere and simple contentment with her role as wife and mom. Kathy and Tim speak at churches and conferences on parenting and marriage. Her sons truly arise and call her blessed. Kathy is also a teacher's aide at our children's school. She is a treasure all around. Kathy has been gracious enough to share this family heirloom recipe with us!

Savory Spoonfuls

1 can cream of mushroom soup

8 oz. cream cheese

¼ cup chopped celery

¼ cup chopped onion

1 envelope unflavored gelatin

1 cup mayo

6 oz. crab meat

Melt soup and cream cheese together. Dissolve gelatin in ¼ cup cold water and add remaining ingredients. Pour into lightly-greased mold. Chill until firm. Serve with crackers.

Manly Game Day Dip

(Photo by Toni Valentini)

Kevin and Penny are a great couple. They prayerfully encourage one another in their individual goals, whether it is fitness or career or talents. Together they love their two daughters with their whole hearts. They first brought this wonderfully-satisfying dip in 2012 and it won with high honors. They generously brought the dip again in 2013 (along with another yummy dip). Kevin and Penny got this recipe from a friend, who got it from another friend. You know a recipe is good when it is shared! We don't know the original source but there are several online recipes that you can Google and tweak yourself to satisfy your taste buds.

This is another easy dip that pleases a crowd...or just a few! Get a hearty cracker and dig in!

Savory Spoonfuls

1 package hot sausage

1 package cream cheese

1 can diced tomatoes

½ diced onion

Brown sausage with onion. Once sausage is cooked thoroughly, add cream cheese and tomatoes. Mix well until blended completely. Serve warm with crackers. Garnish with tomatoes if desired.

Fiery Pig Dip

SerenDIPity 2013 (Photo by Toni Valentini)

Ken is a Philadelphia police officer and a dear friend of my husband and me. Moreover, he is a devoted family man who loves and cherishes his wife, Erika, and their two sons. Ken and Erika are one of the most fun enthusiasts of SerenDIPity. They are wholehearted encouragers, and they come early with smiles to offer assistance and they stay late to enjoy the party afterglow with us. Their dips are always thoughtful, inspiring and fun. In 2013, Ken brought this Fiery Pig Dip that won in the Manly category. Get a glass of ice water to accompany this wonderfully sassy and spicy dip!

Ken's dip was made with "Datil Do It" hot sauce with a recipe on the bottle. Ken doubled the amount of hot sauce and gave it its unique name!

http://www.datildoit.com/recipes.htm

Savory Spoonfuls

1 pound of bacon (cooked and chopped finely)

1 cup mayo

1 cup sour cream

1 ½ Tbs. chipotle hot sauce

1 ½ Tbs. Habanero hot sauce

Mix all ingredients together. Serve right away or refrigerate to serve later.

Philly Cheesesteak Dip

My dear friend, Erika, hit the ball out of the ballpark at our very first SerenDIPity ever in 2010! A fabulous Philly girl herself, she made "Philly Cheesesteak Dip" and put the word "present" in presentation. Her dip and display illustrated her enthusiasm and spunk. Erika herself is a steadfast, dedicated girlfriend and one of the sweetest cheerleaders in my life. I am humbled by her consistent, heartfelt and sincere love. Erika can speak truth with grace to me, and she stands firm in her convictions. She loves the Lord and serves her husband, Ken, and two sons, Austin and Connor, with deep devotion.

Erika's dip is from "The Food In My Beard". Cut a hoagie roll and enjoy the messy goodness!

http://www.thefoodinmybeard.com/2009/11/cheesesteak-dip.html

2 Onions (chopped)

1 Cup of cooked diced beef

¼ Cup of banana peppers

1 Tbl. butter

1 Tbl. flour

Drizzle of oil

1 Cup half and half

1 Cup shredded Cheese

Sauté onions in a little oil until caramelized. In separate pan make a roux with flour and butter. Wisk in half and half. Add cheese and stir until smooth.

Stir in peppers, caramelized onions and beef. Serve warm with chips or sliced hoagie rolls.

Savory Spoonfuls

Vidalia Onion Dip

SerenDIPity 2011 (Photo by Megan Brock)

My friend, Ronna, embodies the scripture "Rejoice with those who rejoice; mourn with those who mourn" from Romans 12:15. Ronna rejoices with passion and genuineness at the accomplishments of her family and friends. She also comes alongside those who are in a difficult season of life and serves the Lord by serving those with hurting hearts. Ronna has been an exuberant guest and supporter of SerenDIPity. Her ebullience makes us want to host SerenDIPity over and over and over.

People are still talking about my friend Ronna's Vidalia Onion Dip from SerenDIPity 2011! This seriously delicious dip is a smash hit because it is not intimidating to make as it contains only a few ingredients, and it is deeeeeeeelicous! It is a crowd-pleasing dip and yet just right for an intimate gathering. Ronna's friend shared this recipe with her several years ago, and it originated from The Food Network. Preheat your oven, whip this dip together and get ready to enjoy! You can serve it with corn chips or another sturdy chip.

http://www.foodnetwork.com/recipes/foodnation-with-bobby-flay/vidalias-favorite-onion-dip-recipe/index.html

"Is there someone that God has put in your path to encourage? Maybe it's through a very unique situation, or maybe the person themselves, is very 'unique'. Ask Him who you could reach out, put your arms around and invite into your home. You might be surprised at the answer you get!"

~ Clare Smith

How precious is Your loving-kindness, O God! Therefore the children of men put their trust under the shadow of Your wings. They are abundantly satisfied with the fullness of Your house, and You give them drink from the river of Your pleasures. For with You is the fountain of life; in Your light we see light."

~ Psalm 36:7-9

Savory Spoonfuls

Sundried Tomato and Feta Torte Dip

Lucille and I have been girlfriends for over twenty years. I am humbled when she introduces me as her "dearest friend". Twenty years of love and nurture and care does that to a friendship – it makes it dear. We've been through mountains and valleys together. We've encouraged each other, prayed for each other, cried with each other, rejoiced with each other. We have seen each other's God-given gifts and cheered one another on as He uses them. We have given each other room to grow, kept each other accountable and challenged one another when necessary. One of Lucille's great gifts is hospitality….and cooking! Lucille can make even a peanut butter and jelly sandwich special.

Lucille's gift of teaching blended together with her culinary talents are the foundation of the God-given ministry she calls "Psalm 34:8 Cooking". While your torte is molding and chilling in the refrigerator, hop on over to see Lucille. She welcomes you with an open door and warm heart. Lucille's recipe requires patience in the preparation, but it is so worth it! Lucille developed this recipe over twenty years with varying ingredients, but has now perfected it. It is a unique savory appetizer in which to dip your favorite pita chip or tortilla chip.

2 8-oz. packages of cream cheese (use organic or best quality you can)

1 stick butter

1 small sweet onion sautéed briefly in olive oil to soften; cool

1 clove garlic, minced very finely

Tabasco and fresh pepper to taste

1/2 cup toasted pine nuts

1 8-oz jar sundried tomatoes in oil, drained and chopped. (Lucille

uses the food processor). If Lucille needs more tomatoes, she will add some rehydrated sundried tomatoes to the oil-packed ones. For the small loaf pan mold, she added another 1/2 cup.

1/2 cup pesto

1. Combine cream cheese, butter, feta, onion, garlic, Tabasco and pepper in bowl of food processor or mixer.

2. Have other ingredients ready for layering: tomatoes, pesto and pine nuts.

3. Lightly grease the mold of your choice and line it with plastic wrap. Be sure the wrap extends past the edge of the mold. Press wrap against sides of your mold. (Lucille used a small loaf pan.)

4. Layer your ingredients in whatever order you like. Lucille uses the following order: cream cheese, pesto, tomatoes, pine nuts. Repeat until your mold is filled.

5. Fold extended plastic wrap on top of last layer.

6. Weight down torte with a heavy object.

7. Refrigerate up to 3 days.

8. When ready to serve, unfold the plastic on top of the mold. Turn mold over and lift off. Remove plastic and serve with your choice of crackers or chips.

Savory Spoonfuls

"How sweet are Your words to my mouth, sweeter than honey to my mouth!"

~ Psalm 119:103

This beautiful tray of cream puffs, cake bars and dips
was made by my friend, Kelly. (Photo by Megan Brock ~ 2011)
(Don't you wish the picture was scratch and sniff?)
To see another sweet creation by Kelly,
go to page 117 for her Caramel Espresso Dip.

Chapter 8

Dollops of Dessert

For all of you sweet tooths out there, this chapter is for you! Sweet dips have taken dessert to a new level. These dips are great if you just want "a little something"…or if you want several little somethings!! Dipping desserts afford you the fun and enjoyment of several different desserts, flavors and textures. Make a cup of coffee and enjoy!

Sweet Dessert Dip Recipes

It's so much fun to see all the creative ways guests prepare their dips, especially sweet dips. At our first SerenDIPity, dessert dips were on the lighter side and it seemed savory dips prevailed. However, our family and friends have become quite imaginative with sweet dips and they are now some of the favorites! Move over savory dips and make room for the sweetness!

SerenDIPity: Celebrating Dips, Faith & Friendship

Dessert Dip Table ~ SerenDIPity 2011
(Photo by Megan Brock)

Dollops of Dessert

Big DIP made by Carol Gallagher. (Photo by Toni Valentini ~ 2012)

My thoughtful friend Carol Gallagher is known for making Rice Krispy's Treats in many shapes, sizes and designs. What a fun serendipity when she brought a big DIP to SerenDIPity in 2012 and again in 2013. We were delighted with the repeat performance!

Carol uses the traditional Rice Krispy's Treats recipe on the Rice Krispy's box (multiplying the ingredients equally as needed depending on what she is making). In Carol's words, "If you butter your hands first, you can form anything!"

Cherry Cheesecake Dip

The now-famous Cherry Cheesecake Dip by Lisa Lohwasser
(Photo by Megan Brock ~ 2011)

My girlfriend, Lisa, and I get the biggest chuckle out of the serendipitous sensation her dip has become! Busy being a wife to her husband, Rich, and a mom to her three young and active boys, and working full-time, Lisa did not have time to plan ahead with a recipe. The day of my SerenDIPity in 2011, she opened her cabinets to see what she could quickly mix together. She wanted an easy yet appealing offering to bring to the party. Seeing a box of Jell-O No Bake Cheesecake Mix in her cabinet, she asked Rich to run to the grocery store and get some Cool Whip, a can of cherry cheesecake filling and a box of graham crackers.

What Lisa literally whipped together that Saturday afternoon has become the most sought after dessert dip! Hundreds, often thousands, of visitors have come to my blog Joy In The Truth for this recipe every week. It has also become a hit on Pinterest. Her last-minute sweet dip creation is a cyber-sensation! All of this is truly a serendipity to Lisa and to me! We had nothing to do with the popularity or promotion of her now-famous Cherry Cheesecake Dip! Here is this easy and delicious recipe!

1 Box of Jell-O No Bake Cheesecake Mix

1 8-ounce tub of Cool Whip

1 21-ounce can of cherry pie filling

(or use any other canned fruit or fresh fruit you desire)

Prepare Jell-O Cheesecake Mix according to directions on box. Stir in the Cool Whip. Place cheesecake mixture on desired serving tray and pour cherry pie filling on top of cheesecake mixture. Chill until ready to serve. Serve with graham crackers or another dipper of your choice.

Cannoli Dip

(Photo by Megan Brock ~ 2011)

My cousin-in-law and friend, Kim, is one of the most wonderful hostesses I know! She and her husband, John, entertain with generous and loving hearts. Going to their home is always an oasis and a pleasure. John and Kim heartily enjoy SerenDIPity each year and always contribute amazing dips. Each year Kim graciously brings her dip on a new unique serving tray and then leaves the tray with me as a hostess gift. I love this idea and have used it now myself.

Kim, inspired by her girlfriend's recipe for Cannoli Dip, made her own version of the dip she originally borrowed from a friend and put a twist on the recipe by using both butter and ricotta cheese along with cream cheese. Blending other flavors and ingredients and truly making this recipe her own, Kim's Cannoli Dip was a big winner at SerenDIPity!

Dollops of Dessert

1 cup powdered sugar

½ stick butter (softened)

1 8-oz. package of cream cheese

1 tsp. vanilla

¼ tsp. cinnamon

½ cup ricotta cheese

½ cup mini semisweet chocolate chips

Mix together all ingredients well, except the chocolate chips.

Once well mixed, fold in the chocolate chips. Serve with pizzelles.

Key Lime Dip

SerenDIPity 2012 ~ (Photo by Toni Valentini)

Kristin is one of those quiet, lovely and steady friends. A loving wife and wonderful home-schooling mom, Kristin inspires me with her intrinsic humility and gentleness. Though I was not the least bit surprised, the first time Kristin and her husband, Trevor, attended SerenDIPity, her Key Lime Dip was a huge hit and won the "Tastiest Dessert Dip" prize!

"...humility brings honor."
Proverbs 29:23(NLT)

Like Kristin, the Key Lime Dip is sweet, unassuming and filled with delightful flavors at the heart of it. Kristin used Kelly and Pam's Key Lime Pie Dip from www.food.com as her base recipe and then added a few twists of her own. Here is the recipe.

Dollops of Dessert

¼ cup key lime juice, plus

2 tablespoons key lime juice

2 (8 ounce) packages light cream cheese

1 (14 ounce) can Eagle Brand Condensed Milk

¼ cup sugar

Whip the cream cheese until it is fluffy. Add the key lime juice and sugar, and then the condensed milk. Continue to mix on high speed until fluffy and combined. Will have the consistency of a thick frosting. Refrigerate, and serve with graham crackers, vanilla wafers, ginger snaps, sliced fruit, etc.

Notes from Kristin:

I used about a ½ cup of key lime juice. It has to be key lime juice, not just regular lime juice. Make sure the cream cheese is softened. I used confectioner's sugar (it doesn't specify in the recipe). I also added the zest from one lime and stirred it into the dip once done mixing the other ingredients. You can garnish with lime or lime zest as well. I did use graham crackers, vanilla wafers, ginger snaps for dipping. Fresh fruit would be fabulous as well!

Chocolate Mousse Dip

My friend Cathi is a rich treasure in my life. Confident and content, she is most comfortable staying out of any limelight. She effortlessly demonstrates her faithfulness in friendship by praying with discernment and by speaking truth with love and grace and boldness. Her walk with the Lord and her testimony give her a rare textured depth. I love her heart for the Lord and for family and friends.

Cathi's Chocolate Mousse Dip won rave reviews at SerenDIPity. Her delicious dessert dip was inspired by the Coffee Ricotta Mousse recipe from Moosewood Restaurant Cooks at Home book (page 307). You'll want to make this one! Here's the recipe.

1 pound ricotta cheese

½ cup confectioner's sugar

2 tablespoons instant coffee granules

½ teaspoon pure vanilla extract

1 tablespoon brandy (optional)

In bowl of a food processor or using an electric mixer, whip all of the ingredients together until smooth and evenly colored. Serve immediately or cover and refrigerate until serving.

(Cathi served hers in a large bowl with butter cookies for dipping.)

Dollops of Dessert

Chocolate Chip Cheese Ball

Laura and I met when my son, Joshua, and her daughter, Alexa, were in pre-kindergarten together at a local Christian school. She still gets a giggle that I wrote her a hand-written note the first time I invited her and her children over for a play date. That's how Laura and I roll. We love each other for who God has made us and how He is transforming us. We can laugh at ourselves (and at each other) together. Laura is one of those friends where we never miss a beat. We could not talk for several weeks, and we will just hit the ground running and pick up where we left off. Always a lady, Laura speaks with love, refreshing honesty and will fiercely defend truth. She is on the side of truth. I am so thankful for her. *"Jesus answered, 'You are right in saying I am a king. In fact, for this reason I was born, and for this I came into the world, to testify to the truth. Everyone on the side of truth listens to Me.'" (John 18:37 NIV)*

Laura brought a Chocolate Chip Cheese Ball to the first ever SerenDIPity and it was a crowd pleaser! Laura found the recipe at www.allrecipes.com and served it with apple slices, graham crackers and pretzels. Put these ingredients on your shopping list! Your guests will love it!

http://allrecipes.com/recipe/chocolate-chip-cheese-ball/

The law of the Lord is perfect, refreshing the soul.
The statutes of the Lord are trustworthy, making wise the simple.
The precepts of the Lord are right, giving joy to the heart.
The commands of the Lord are radiant, giving light to the eyes.
The fear of the Lord is pure, enduring forever.
The decrees of the Lord are firm, and all of them are righteous.
They are more precious than gold, than much pure gold;
they are sweeter than honey, than honey from the honeycomb.
By them your servant is warned; in keeping them there is great reward.
~ Psalm 19:7-11

SerenDIPity: Celebrating Dips, Faith & Friendship

How sweet are your words to my taste, sweeter than honey to my mouth!

~ Psalm 119:103

Caramel Espresso Dip

Kelly made this scrumptious Caramel Espresso Dip for SerenDIPity 2013. A variety of her own homemade biscotti were the dipping tools! Wowzie! Let's just say she graciously put the leftovers in our refrigerator and we enjoyed them the next morning as a special breakfast treat. Dessert for breakfast…great way to start the day! SCRUMPTUOUS!

Kelly's dip was inspired by http://food52.com/recipes/8956-caramel-tiramisu-dip. She changed it a bit to fit her taste and the taste of the guest. I love this recipe because it is just a few ingredients too delicious!!!

¾ cup caramel sauce

1 cup whipped cream

8 oz. mascarpone cheese

1 Tbs. Instant espresso

1-1/2 tsp. vanilla extract

Whip all ingredients together and sprinkle extra espresso granules on top for garnish.

Refrigerate until serving. Refrigerate leftovers.

Chapter 9

SerenDIPity Afterglow

"In the same way, let your light shine before others, that they may see your good deeds and glorify your Father in heaven."

~ Matthew 5:16

Stepping Out With SerenDIPity

"…whoever is kind to the needy honors God."

~ Proverbs 14:31

Sometimes God blesses in the most personal ways that are treasures just between us and Him. A word He whispers to our hearts, an answered private prayer, a perfect provision to meet a specific need. Often we keep these as quiet treasures we ponder in our hearts.

But I believe most blessings are to be shared for His glory and for His name's sake. That is one of the main reasons I was spurred on to write this book. When God blesses us, with thankfulness unto Him, we look for ways to bless others with what He has given us.

So as this book comes to a close, I invite you to consider how you can share SerenDIPity. As a family, we are looking and excited for ways we can pour blessings on others through SerenDIPity. Here are a few ideas we have. Let us know your unique ideas, too!

- Host a SerenDIPity in your home for your neighborhood.
- Host a SerenDIPity outside as a block party.
- Bring a SerenDIPity party to a retirement home with dips that would be appealing to older men and women. Spend time dipping hours away with them.
- Bring a SerenDIPity party to an orphanage. You will bring such smiles to the children's hearts as you share your love and dips. You can make child-friendly dips such as peanut butter and jelly dip, hoagie dip, cookie dough dip and fruit dip.
- Host a SerenDIPity for your children's friends.
- Treat your children's teachers and staff to a SerenDIPity lunch at Christmas time during National Teacher Appreciation Week or at the end of the school year.
- Have a SerenDIPity dinner night for your family with a blend of savory and sweet dips. They will love it and look forward to it again!

Just as you are on the lookout for God's serendipities in your life, look for ways to bring His joy to those around you.

> *"Your situation may be as hot and barren as a desert or as forlorn and meaningless as a wasteland…But all I ask is that you…be on the lookout. God may very well be planning a serendipity in your life."*
>
> *~ Charles R. Swindoll*

Dip Your Heart In!

"I will delight myself in Your statutes; I will not neglect Your word."

~ Psalm 119:16

I am a forever-student of the Bible. I do delight in God's Word. One of my greatest joys in writing this little book is having blended His Word in throughout. I pray that if you are not acquainted with Scripture that you are drawn to open His Word and dip your heart in the streams of living water.

If you do know God's Word but have strayed away from daily devotion time, I pray the Scriptures you have read on these pages have whet your appetite such as that you would hunger and thirst for His truths again every day.

If you do not have a Bible, you can read it online at www.blueletterbible.org or www.biblegateway.org. You can also ask your local church for a Bible. If you find yourself unable to get a Bible in your hands, please email me at sharon@seredipitydipsbook.com.

Delighted (Not Always Delightful!)

Yes, I do delight in His Word. But it should go without saying ~ that doesn't mean that I am always delightful! I can be crotchety. I get grumpy. When I am tired, I get downright unlovely. So I am very thankful for my family who loves me with grace, truth and great senses of humor.

God's Word is truth and life. I know that with my whole heart. His Words are on these pages and on my lips because I desperately need them myself. Apart from Him, our hearts are desperately wicked. ***"The heart is deceitful above all things, and desperately wicked; Who can know it?" (Jeremiah 17:9)*** I honestly believe that His truths, when soaked into our hearts and lived out through our actions and responses, are the only thing that will truly minister to any of us.

May my tongue sing of Your word,
for all Your commands are righteous.

Psalm 119:172

God's Word, His written expression of Himself, is central to me because of my own awareness of my desperate heart. Life is challenging. Even a blessed life is challenging. His truths are the anchor to my soul. **"We have this hope as an anchor for the soul, firm and secure." (Hebrews 6:19)**

Rarely do I send a greeting card or an email to a friend without a scripture in it. I want to write His Word on the doorframes of our hearts, homes and relationships. **"These commandments that I give you today are to be upon your hearts. Impress them on your children. Talk about them when you sit at home and when you walk along the road, when you lie down and when you get up. Tie them as symbols on your hands and bind them on your foreheads. Write them on the doorframes of your houses and on your gates." (Deuteronomy 6:6-9)**

Those who know and love me well know that I love His Word because it is life and I want it to judge the thoughts and attitudes of my own heart. God is so good to have given me a husband and friends who will share a scripture with me that I need to hear…whether for encouragement or conviction. My favorite Psalm is 119, said to be a devotional on the Word of God. **"Your Word has given me life." (Psalm 119:50)**

Because my not-always-so-delightful self delights in God's Word, some may misunderstand my heart. Know that I am broken before the Lord every day. One of the loveliest things a friend has ever said to me is *"You are broken before the Lord even when you are in a season of blessing."* Oh friends, if that is true at all, it is only by His grace and because I know God is God. I know my desperate need for Him every moment.

> **The LORD IS CLOSE TO THE BROKENHEARTED**
> *and saves those who are crushed in spirit.*
> *~ Psalm 34:18*

His Word instructs, commands, encourages, comforts, convicts. So, as long as I have breath, I pray His Word is always my delight. And even when I am not so delightful, I pray I always write, speak, sing and live His Word.

> *"For the word of God is living and active.*
> *Sharper than any double-edged sword,*
> *it penetrates even to dividing soul and spirit,*
> *joints and marrow;*
> *it judges the thoughts and attitudes of the heart."*
>
> *Hebrews 4:12*

As you close this book, my prayer is that your heart is encouraged in His truths, that you are spurred on and given to hospitality, that He blesses the friendships He has given you, that He establishes and blesses the work of your heart and hands, and that you dip deep into the riches of the risen Christ through His living word.

Sweet SerenDIPity!

> *"Yet He has not left himself without testimony:*
> *He has shown kindness...*
> *He provides you with plenty of food*
> *and fills your hearts with joy."*
>
> *~ Acts 14:17*

Notes

The Serendipity logo was designed by my friend Tracy Stokes.
https://www.facebook.com/tracy.stokes.587

SerenDIPity pictures taken by:

(2012 and 2013) Toni Valentini
https://www.facbook.com/nowpicturethis

(2011) Megan Petock Brock
http://www.megbrock.com/

(2010) Heather Beals
http://bealsonwheels.blogspot.com/
and http://www.ourlittleladybugs.blogspot.com/

Made in the USA
Charleston, SC
18 November 2013